6-

The Little Big Book of
LOVE

To: _____

From: _____

the little
big book of
LOVE

Edited by **Lena Tabori**
& **Natasha Tabori Fried**

Designed by **Timothy Shaner**

**welcome
BOOKS**

NEW YORK • SAN FRANCISCO

For Franco - L.T.

Published in 2008 by Welcome Books®
An Imprint of Welcome Enterprises, Inc.
6 West 18th Street, New York, NY 10011
Tel: 212-989-3200; Fax: 212-989-3205
www.welcomebooks.com

Publisher: Lena Tabori
Project Director: Natasha Tabori Fried
Art Director: Gregory Wakabayashi
Designer: Timothy Shaner
Jacket & Case Designer: Amanda Webster
Project Assistant: Kara Mason

Library of Congress Cataloging-in-Publication Data
The little big book of love / edited by Lena Tabori ; designed by Timothy Shaner.
p.cm.
ISBN 0-688-17415-9
1. Love quotations, maxims, etc. 2. St. Valentine's Day Miscellanea.
3. Love Literary collections. I. Tabori, Lena.
PN6084.L6L57 2000
302.3—dc2   99-44175
CIP

ISBN 978-1-59962-052-7

Printed in China
FIRST EDITION
2 4 6 8 10 9 7 5 3 1

Contents

Contents

Poetry

Contents

Contents

Recipes

Songs

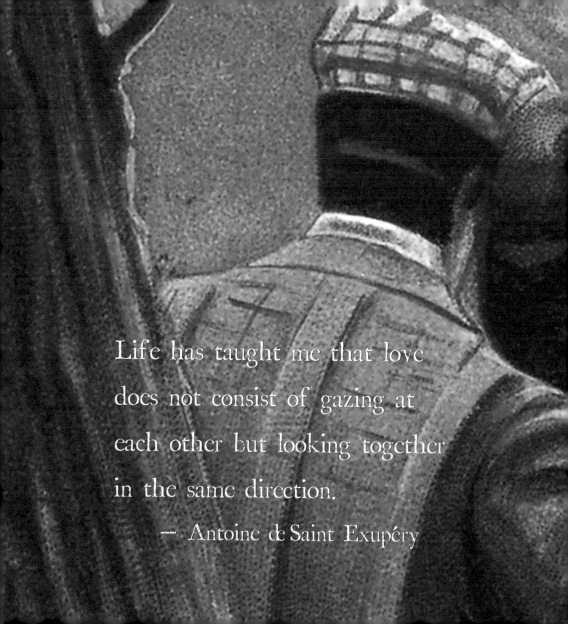

Life has taught me that love does not consist of gazing at each other but looking together in the same direction.

— Antoine de Saint Exupéry

Foreword

O h, gosh. I am about to be sixty-four and the Beatles immediately come to mind. My generation thought sixty-four was old. They didn't realize how young we were to be. They didn't imagine Mick Jagger and Abbie Hoffman and Gloria Steinem. But here we are still alive, still in love, still passionate—and we haven't forgotten any of what came before either.

This brilliant little love anthology was originally published nine years ago. I had just fallen in love with the man I still live with. And yes, he stills needs me and I still feed him. Now the rights to this really nice book are back with a publishing house I run and we are revising it a bit (not much) and publishing it again. It is so classic.

When I was first working on it, flying Jet Blue back and forth to be with this terrifically nice man I met in Kauai, I was reading Rumi:

"When I am with you, we stay up all night.
When you are not here, I can't go to sleep.
Praise God for these two insomnias!
And the difference between them."

And, I laughed thinking how wonderfully specific someone else's experience can be to my own. This book is filled with that repeating recognition.

One of my daughters, now thirty-six, and I read, talked, and shared with

13

Foreword

each other material that we loved. She rediscovered Jane Austen and Charlotte Bronte. I discovered Nikki Giovanni and Simon Ortiz. We tossed anything we didn't both love and anything which the delicious, merry, and very turn-of-the-century illustrations didn't resonate to. The images now marry brilliantly to everything from *The Velveteen Rabbit* to Napoleon's jealous letters to his wife Josephine, from the songs of Cole Porter and the Gershwin brothers to the plays of Shakespeare. The illustrations adore their association with the recipes, and soar with the poems. The art is key to this volume's charm.

This book believes that love is here to stay. It is packed with all the diversity that mostly the Western world has had to offer. Johnny Mercer's *Something's Gotta Give* is certainly different than Robert Frost's *Never Again Would Bird's Song be the Same* and, artistically, bears no resemblance to e.e.cummings' *Somewhere I Have Never Travelled* but each of these creators is celebrating the loved one. Mark Twain's ever-perfect *Adam and Eve* ("We?" says Adam "Where did I get that word? —I remember now—the new creature uses It.") sets the tone for the book's commitment. "He" discovers "she" in this divine piece and, complicated as the discovery was and often is, he cannot live without her.

This fat little book is overflowing with love. It is in love with love. Love at its deepest, highest, most touching place. Oh, yes, there is some obsession: Cole Porter's *Night and Day* speaks of it and Sarah Bernhardt celebrates it and the aphrodisiac dinner even attempts to instigate it. And, there is certainly passion. There is also tenderness and humor. Love has a way of bringing everyone to the same place and when Queen Victoria confides of her love for the commoner Albert, whom she marries, you come to the heart of the book. And, you find this commitment spoken in endless ways: in Robert Bly' s exquisite *Such Different*

Foreword

Wants and in the amazing letters that Winston Churchill, John Adams, Tsar Nicholas, and Robert Browning wrote to their wives.

Finally, there are the perfect recipes: chocolate mousse, fortune cookies complete with suggested fortunes, and unbelievable lemon hearts. A Forgiveness Breakfast will occasionally be in order and it, too, is here. But mainly, primarily, there is our hope that you will find this vibrant little book filled with profound and wonderful surprises.

To you, from Natasha and me,
   Lena Tabori

He Wishes for
the Cloths of Heaven

William Butler Yeats

Had I the heavens' embroidered cloths,
Enwrought with golden and silver light,
The blue and the dim and the dark cloths
Of night and light and the half-light,
I would spread the cloths under your feet:
But I, being poor, have only my dreams;
I have spread my dreams under your feet;
Tread softly because you tread on my dreams.

The Diary of Adam and Eve

Mark Twain

PART I
EXTRACTS FROM ADAM'S DIARY

MONDAY   This new creature with the long hair is a good deal in the way. It is always hanging around and following me about. I don't like this; I am not used to company. I wish it would stay with the other animals. . . . Cloudy today, wind in the east; think we shall have rain. . . *We?* Where did I get that word?—I remember now—the new creature uses it.

TUESDAY   Been examining the great waterfall. It is the finest thing on the estate, I think. The new creature calls it Niagara Falls—why, I am sure I do not know. Says it *looks* like Niagara Falls. That is not a reason, it is mere waywardness and imbecility. I get no chance to name anything myself. The new creature names everything that comes along, before I can get in a protest. And always the same pretext is offered—it *looks* like the thing. There is the dodo, for instance. Says the moment one looks at it one sees at a glance that it "looks like a dodo." It will have to keep that name, no doubt. It wearies me to fret about it, and it does no good, anyway. Dodo! It looks no more like a dodo than I do.

FRIDAY   The naming goes recklessly on, in spite of anything I can do. I had a very good name for the estate, and it was musical and pretty—*Garden of Eden*. Privately, I continue to call it that, but not any longer publicly. The new creature says it is all woods and rocks and scenery, and therefore has no resemblance to a garden. Says it *looks* like a park, and does not look like anything *but* a park. Consequently, without consulting me, it has been new-named—*Niagara Falls Park*. This is sufficiently high-handed, it seems to me. And already there is a sign up:

Keep Off The Grass

My life is not as happy as it was.

SATURDAY   The new creature eats too much fruit. We are going to run short, most likely. "We" again—that is *its* word; mine, too, now, from hearing it so much. Good deal of fog this morning. I do not go out in the fog myself. The new creature does. It goes out in all weathers, and stumps right in with its muddy feet. And talks. It used to be so pleasant and quiet here.

SUNDAY   Pulled through. This day is getting to be more and more trying. It was selected and set apart last November as a day of rest. I had already six of them per week before. This morning found the new creature trying to clod apples out of that forbidden tree.

MONDAY   The new creature says its name is Eve. That is all right, I have

21

no objections. Says it is to call it by, when I want it to come. I said it was superfluous, then. The word evidently raised me in its respect; and indeed it is a large, good word and will bear repetition. It says it is not an It, it is a She. This is probably doubtful; yet it is all one to me; what she is were nothing to me if she would but go by herself and not talk.

TUESDAY   She told me she was made out of a rib taken from my body. This is at least doubtful, if not more than that. I have not missed any rib. . . She is in much trouble about the buzzard; says grass does not agree with it; is afraid she can't raise it; thinks it was intended to live on decayed flesh. The buzzard must get along the best it can with what it is provided. We cannot overturn the whole scheme to accommodate the buzzard.

SUNDAY   Pulled through.

TUESDAY   She has taken up with a snake now. The other animals are glad, for she was always experimenting with them and bothering them; and I am glad because the snake talks, and this enables me to get a rest.

FRIDAY   She says the snake advises her to try the fruit of that tree, and says the result will be a great and fine and noble education. I told her there would be another result, too—it would introduce death into the world. That was a mistake—it had been better to keep the remark to myself; it only gave her an idea—she could save the sick buzzard, and furnish fresh meat to the despondent lions and tigers. I advised her to keep away from the tree. She said she wouldn't. I foresee trouble. Will emigrate.

WEDNESDAY   I have had a variegated time. I escaped last night, and rode a

22

horse all night as fast as he could go, hoping to get clear out of the Park and hide in some other country before the trouble should begin; but it was not to be. About an hour after sun-up, as I was riding through a flowery plain where thousands of animals were grazing, slumbering, or playing with each other, according to their wont, all of a sudden they broke into a tempest of frightful noises, and in one moment the plain was a frantic commotion and every beast was destroying its neighbor. I knew what it meant—Eve had eaten that fruit, and death was come into the world. . . The tigers ate my horse, paying no attention when I ordered them to desist, and they would have eaten me if I had stayed— which I didn't, but went away in much haste. . . I found this place, outside the Park, and was fairly comfortable for a few days, but she has found me out. Found me out, and has named the place

Tonawanda—says it *looks* like that. In fact I was sorry she came, for there are but meager pickings here, and she brought some of those apples. I was obliged to eat them, I was so hungry. It was against my principles, but I find that principles have no real force except when one is well fed. . . She came curtained in boughs and bunches of leaves, and when I asked her what she meant by such nonsense, and snatched them away and threw them down, she tittered and blushed. I had never seen a person titter and blush before, and to me it seemed unbecoming and idiotic. She said I would

soon know how it was myself. This was correct. Hungry as I was, I laid down the apple half-eaten—certainly the best one I ever saw, considering the lateness of the season—and arrayed myself in the discarded boughs and branches, and then spoke to her with some severity and ordered her to go and get some more and not make such a spectacle of herself. She did it, and after this we crept down to where the wild-beast battle had been, and collected some skins, and I made her patch together a couple of suits proper for public occasions. They are uncomfortable, it is true, but stylish, and that is the main point about clothes. . . I find she is a good deal of a companion. I see I should be lonesome and depressed without her, now that I have lost my property. Another thing, she says it is ordered that we work for our living hereafter. She will be useful. I will superintend.

NEXT YEAR   We have named it Cain. She caught it while I was up country trapping on the North Shore of the Erie; caught it in the timber a couple of miles from our dug-out—or it might have been four, she isn't certain which. It resembles us in some ways, and may be a relation. That is what she thinks, but this is an error, in my judgment. The difference in size warrants the conclusion that it is a different and new kind of animal—a fish, perhaps, though when I put it in the water to see, it sank, and she plunged in and snatched it out before there was opportunity for the experiment to determine the matter. I still think it is a fish, but she is indifferent about what it is, and will not let me have it to try. I do not understand this. The coming of the creature seems to have changed her whole nature and made her unreasonable about experiments. She thinks more of it than she does of any of the other animals, but is not able to explain why. Her mind is disordered—everything shows it. Sometimes she carries the fish in her arms half the night when it complains and wants to get to the water. At such times the water comes out of the places in her face that she looks out of, and she pats the fish on the back and makes soft sounds with her mouth to soothe it, and betrays sorrow and solicitude in a hundred ways. I have never seen her do like this with any other fish, and it troubles me greatly. She used to carry the young tigers around so, and play with them, before we lost our property, but it was only play; she never took on about them like this when their dinner disagreed with them.

SUNDAY She doesn't work, Sundays, but lies around all tired out, and likes to have the fish wallow over her; and she makes fool noises to amuse it, and pretends to chew its paws, and that makes it laugh. I have not seen a fish before that could laugh. This makes me doubt. . . I have come to like Sunday myself. Superintending all the week tires a body so. There ought to be more Sundays. In the old days they were tough, but now they come handy.

THREE MONTHS LATER The perplexity augments instead of diminishing. I sleep but little. It has ceased from lying around, and goes about on its four legs now. Yet it differs from the other four-legged animals, in that its front legs are unusually short, consequently this causes the main part of its person to stick up uncomfortably high in the air, and this is not attractive. It is built much as we are, but its method of traveling shows that it is not of our breed. The short front legs and long hind ones indicate that it is of the kangaroo family, but it is a marked

26

variation of the species, since the true kangaroo hops; whereas this one never does. Still it is a curious and interesting variety, and has not been catalogued before. As I discovered it, I have felt justified in securing the credit of the discovery by attaching my name to it, and hence have called it *Kangaroorum Adamiensis*. . . . It must have been a young one when it came, for it has grown exceedingly since. It must be five times as big, now, as it was then, and when discontented it is able to make from twenty-two to thirty-eight times the noise it made at first. As already observed, I was not at home when it first came, and she told me she found in the woods. It seems odd that it should be the only one, yet it must be so, for I have worn myself out these many weeks trying to find another one to add to my collection, and for this one to play with; for surely then it would be quieter and we could tame it more easily. But I find none, nor any vestige of any; and strangest of all, no tracks. It has to live on the ground, it cannot help itself; therefore, how does it get about without leaving a track? I have set a dozen traps, but they do no good.

FIVE MONTHS LATER   It is not a kangaroo. No, for it supports itself by holding to her finger, and thus goes a few steps on its hind legs, and then falls down. It is probably some kind of a bear; and yet it has no tail—as yet—and no fur, except on its head. It still keeps on growing—that is a curious circumstance, for bears get their growth earlier than this. Bears are dangerous—since our catastrophe—and I shall not be satisfied to have this one prowling about the place much longer without a muzzle on. I have offered to get her a kangaroo if she would let this one go, but it did no good—she is determined to run us into all sorts of foolish risks, I think. She was not like this before she lost her mind.

A FORTNIGHT LATER   I examined its mouth. There is no danger yet: it has only one tooth. It has no tail yet. It makes more noise now than it ever did before—and mainly at night. I have moved out. But I shall go over, mornings, to breakfast, and see if it has more teeth. If it gets a mouthful of teeth it will be time for it to go, tail or no tail, for a bear does not need a tail in order to be dangerous.

FOUR MONTHS LATER   I have been off hunting and fishing a month, up in the region that she calls Buffalo; I don't know why, unless it is because there are not any buffaloes there. Meantime the bear has learned to paddle around all by itself on its hind legs, and says "poppa" and "momma." It is certainly a new species. This resemblance to words may be purely accidental, of course, and may have no purpose or meaning; but even in that case it is still extraordinary, and is a thing which no other bear can do. This imitation of speech, taken together with general absence of fur and entire absence of tail, sufficiently indicates that this is a new kind of bear. The further study of it will be exceedingly interesting. Meantime I will go off on a far expedition among the forests of the north and make an exhaustive search. There must certainly be another one somewhere, and this one will be less dangerous when it has company of its own species. I will go straightway; but I will muzzle this one first.

THREE MONTHS LATER It has been a weary, weary hunt, yet I have had no success. In the mean time, without stirring from the home estate, she has caught another one! I never saw such luck. I might have hunted these woods a hundred years, I never would have run across that thing.

NEXT DAY I have been comparing the new one with the old one, and it is perfectly plain that they are the same breed. I was going to stuff one of them for my collection, but she is prejudiced against it for some reason or other; so I have relinquished the idea, though I think it is a mistake. It would be an irreparable loss to science if they should get away. The old one is tamer than it

was and can laugh and talk like the parrot, having learned this, no doubt, from being with the parrot so much, and having the imitative faculty in a highly developed degree. I shall be astonished if it turns out to be a new kind of parrot; and yet I ought not to be astonished, for it has already been everything else it could think of since those first days when it was a fish. The new one is as ugly now as the old one was at first; has the same sulphur-and-raw-meat complexion and the same singular head without any fur on it. She calls it Abel.

TEN YEARS LATER They are *boys*; we found it out long ago. It was their coming in that small, immature shape that puzzled us; we were not used to it. There are some girls now. Abel is a good boy, but if Cain had stayed a bear it would have improved him. After all these years, I see that I was mistaken about Eve in the beginning; it is better to live outside the Garden with her than inside it without her. At first I thought she talked too much; but now I should be sorry to have that voice fall silent and pass out of my life. Blessed be the chestnut that brought us near together and taught me to know the goodness of her heart and the sweetness of her spirit!

PART II
EVE'S DIARY

AFTER THE FALL   When I look back, the Garden is a dream to me. It was beautiful, surpassingly beautiful, enchantingly beautiful; and now it is lost, and I shall not see it any more.

The Garden is lost, but I have found *him*, and am content. He loves me as well as he can; I love him with all the strength of my passionate nature, and this, I think, is proper to my youth and sex. If I ask myself why I love him, I find I do not know, and do not really much care to know; so I suppose that this kind of love is not a product of reasoning and statistics, like one's love for other reptiles and animals. I think that this must be so. I love certain birds because of their song; but I do not love Adam on account of his singing—no, it is not that; the more he sings the more I do not get reconciled to it. Yet I ask him to sing, because I wish to learn to like everything he is interested in. I am sure I can learn, because at first I could not stand it, but now I can. It sours the milk, but it doesn't matter; I can get used to that kind of milk.

It is not on account of his brightness that I love him—no, it is not that. He is not to blame for his brightness, such as it is, for he did not make it himself; he is as God made him, and that is sufficient. There was a wise purpose in it, *that* I

know. In time it will develop, though I think it will not be sudden; and besides, there is no hurry; he is well enough just as he is.

It is not on account of his gracious and considerate ways and his delicacy that I love him. No, he has lacks in these regards, but he is well enough just so, and is improving.

It is not on account of his industry that I love him—no, it is not that. I think he has it in him, and I do not know why he conceals it from me. It is my only pain. Otherwise he is frank and open with me, now. I am sure he keeps nothing from me but this. It grieves me that he should have a secret from me, and sometimes it spoils my sleep, thinking about it, but I will put it out of my mind; it shall not trouble my happiness, which is otherwise full to overflowing.

It is not on account of his education that I love him—no, it is not that. He is self-educated, and does really know a multitude of things, but they are not so.

It is not on account of his chivalry that I love him—no, it is not that. He told on me, but I do not blame him; it is a peculiarity of sex, I think, and he did not make his sex. Of course I would not have told on him, I would have perished first; but that is a peculiarity of sex, too, and I do not take credit for it, for I did not make my sex.

Then why is it that I love him? *Merely because he is masculine*, I think.

At bottom he is good, and I love him

32

for that, but I could love him without it. If he should beat me and abuse me, I should go on loving him. I know it. It is a matter of sex, I think.

He is strong and handsome, and I love him for that, and I admire him and am proud of him, but I could love him without those qualities. If he were plain, I should love him; if he were a wreck, I should love him; and I would work for him, and slave over him, and pray for him, and watch by his bedside until I died.

Yes, I think I love him merely because he is *mine* and is *masculine.* There is no other reason, I suppose. And so I think it is as I first said; that this kind of love is not a product of reasonings and statistics. It just *comes*—none knows whence—and cannot explain itself. And doesn't need to.

It is what I think. But I am only a girl, and the first that has examined this matter, and it may turn out that in my ignorance and inexperience, I have not got it right.

FORTY YEARS LATER It is my prayer, it is my longing, that we may pass from this life together—a longing which shall never perish from the earth, but shall have place in the heart of every wife that loves, until the end of time; and it shall be called by my name.

But if one of us must go first, it is my prayer that is shall be I; for he is strong, I am weak, I am not so necessary to him as he is to me—life without him would not be life; how could I endure it? This prayer is also immortal, and will not cease from being offered up while my race continues. I am the first wife; and in the last wife I shall be repeated.

AT EVE'S GRAVE   Adam: Wheresoever she was, *there* was Eden.

34

Never Again Would Birds' Song Be the Same

Robert Frost

He would declare and could himself believe
That the birds there in all the garden round
From having heard the daylong voice of Eve
Had added to their own an oversound,
Her tone of meaning but without the words.
Admittedly an eloquence so soft
Could only have had an influence on birds
When call or laughter carried it aloft.
Be that as may be, she was in their song.
Moreover her voice upon their voices crossed
Had now persisted in the woods so long
That probably it never would be lost.
Never again would birds' song be the same.
And to do that to birds was why she came.

The Forgiveness Breakfast

Breakfast in bed served on a tray covered in rose petals—yellow for jealousy, white for innocence—is an eloquent apology. Red rose petals say "I love you forever." A peony signifies shame.

Strawberry crepes
Bacon
Fresh squeezed orange juice
Champagne
Mocha coffee

1. Prepare crepe batter and refrigerate.
2. Make the coffee.
3. Put the bacon in a shallow pan in the oven for 20-25 minutes at 375°F (turn bacon and pour fat off after ten minutes).
4. Prepare tray with rose petals, cloth napkin, beautiful glasses for juice and champagne (depending on the degree of forgiveness, Dom Perignon will yield the most profound results; Veuve Clicquot is a close second), and a generous cup for the coffee.
5. Squeeze oranges for juice.
6. Prepare crepe filling.
7. Make crepes, pour juice, champagne, and coffee.
8. Look sorry.

Strawberry Crepes

Makes 4 crepes, two for each of you.

CREPES
3/4 cup white all-purpose flour
1 tablespoon sugar
1 egg, slightly beaten
3/4 cup milk
2 tablespoons melted butter

1. Turn the oven on to warm.
2. Sift the flour and sugar in a bowl.
3. Combine the remaining ingredients and pour into the flour.
4. Whisk until smooth. Refrigerate 30 minutes.
5. Heat crepe pan over high heat, and coat pan well with a little butter.
6. Pour 1/4 cup of the batter into the center of the pan and swirl it around until it covers the bottom of the pan.
7. Turn when the edges begin to curl (about 30 seconds).

8. Cook other side about 30 seconds, remove to a plate in the heated oven, cover with another plate while you make the next crepe, and so on.

FILLING

    1 tablespoon butter
    1 tablespoon sugar
    1 tablespoon orange juice
    1 cup small curd cottage cheese
    1 cup sliced strawberries, sprinkled
       with brown sugar

1. Melt butter in a small pan. Add sugar and orange juice, stirring over a low flame until sugar dissolves. Stir in the cottage cheese.

2. Spoon 1/4 cup of the filling in a line down the center of the crepe and sprinkle with 1/4 of the strawberries. Fold one side of the crepe over the filling and berries, then roll the crepe. Garnish with sliced berries and a sprinkling of brown sugar.

Mocha Coffee

    3 tablespoons chocolate syrup
    dash of cinnamon
    1 cup of coffee
    dollop of whipping cream (if you make your own, buy a pint of heavy cream, stir in 2 tablespoons of sugar, and whip on top speed until it forms peaks but before cream turns to butter)

1. Pour syrup and cinnamon into coffee, stir well, and top with cream.

How Do I Love Thee?
Elizabeth Barrett Browning

How do I love thee? Let me count the ways.
I love thee to the depth and breadth and height
My soul can reach, when feeling out of sight
For the ends of Being and ideal Grace.
I love thee to the level of everyday's
Most quiet need, by sun and candle-light.
I love thee freely, as men strive for Right;
I love thee purely, as they turn from Praise.
I love thee with the passion put to use
In my old griefs, and with my childhood's faith.
I love thee with a love I seemed to lose
With my lost saints!—I love thee with the breath,
Smiles, tears, of all my life!—and, if God choose,
I shall but love thee better after death.

Something's Gotta Give

Johnny Mercer

When an irresistible force such as you
Meets an old imovable object like me,
You can bet as sure as you live,
Something's gotta give, something's gotta give, something's gotta give.

When an irrespressible smile such as yours
Warms an implacable heart such as mine,
Don't say no because I insist
Somewhere, somehow, someone's gonna be kissed.

So en garde, who knows what the fates have in store,
From their vast mysterious sky?
I'll try hard ignoring those lips I adore
But how long can anyone try?

Fight, fight, fight, fight, fight, fight it with all of our might,
Chances are some heavenly star spangled night,
We'll find out as sure as we live,
Something's gotta give, something's gotta give, something's gotta give.

Letters between John Adams and his wife, Abigail

TO JOHN   16 October 1774.

My much loved Friend,

I dare not express to you, at three hundred miles' distance, how ardently I long for your return. I have some very miserly wishes, and cannot consent to your spending one hour in town, till, at least, I have had you twelve. The idea plays about my heart, unnerves my hand, whilst I write,—awakens all the tender sentiments, that years have increased and matured, and which, when with me, were every day dispensing to you. The whole collected stock of ten weeks' absence knows not how to brook any longer restraint, but will break forth and flow through my pen.

TO ABIGAIL   June 1777.

Next month completes three years that I have been devoted to the

service of liberty. A slavery it has been to me, whatever the world may think of it. To a man whose attachments to his family are as strong as mine, absence alone from such a wife and such children would be a great sacrifice. But in addition to this separation what have I not done? What have I not suffered? What have I not hazarded? These are questions that I may ask you, but I will ask such questions of none else. Let the cymbals of popularity tinkle still. Let the butterflies of fame glitter with their wings. I shall envy neither their music nor their colors. The loss of property affects me little. All other hard things I despise, but the loss of your company and that of my dear babes for so long a time, I consider as a loss of so much solid happiness. The tender social feelings of my heart which have distressed me beyond all utterance in my most busy active scenes as well as in the numerous hours of melancholy solitude, are known only to God and my own soul.

Abigail and John Adams

TO JOHN

My Dearest Friend,   23 December 1792.

...should I draw you the picture of my heart it would be what I hope you would still love though it contained nothing new. The early possession you obtained there, and the absolute power you have obtained over it, leaves not the smallest space unoccupied. I look back to the early days of our acquaintance and friendship as to the days of love and innocence, and, with an indescribable pleasure, I have seen near a score of years roll over our heads with an affection heightened and improved by time, nor have the dreary years of absence in the smallest degree effaced from my mind the image of the dear untitled man to whom I gave my heart.

John Adams, second president of the United States, married Abigail Adams in October 1764 after a brief courtship. They were happily married for 54 years.

Shall I compare thee to a summer's day?
Thou art more lovely and more temperate:
Rough winds do shake the darling buds of May,
And summer's lease hath all too short a date:
Sometime too hot the eye of heaven shines,
And often is his gold complexion dimm'd;
And every fair from fair sometime declines,
By chance or nature's changing course untrimm'd;
But thy eternal summer shall not fade,
Nor lose possession of that fair thou owest;
Nor shall Death brag thou wander'st in his shade,
When in eternal lines to time thou grow'st:
  So long as men can breathe, or eyes can see,
  So long lives this, and this gives life to thee.

         — William Shakespeare

Sir Gawain

(from *King Arthur and His Knights*)
Thomas Bulfinch

Sir Gawain was nephew to King Arthur, by his sister Morgana, married to Lot, king of Orkney, who was by Arthur made king of Norway. Sir Gawain was one of the most famous knights of the Round Table, and is characterized by the romancers as the *sage* and *courteous* Gawain. To this Chaucer alludes in his "Squiere's Tale," where the strange knight "salueth" all the court

"With so high reverence and observance,
As well in speeche as in countenance,

That Gawain, with his olde curtesie,
Though he were come agen out of faërie,
Ne coude him not amenden with a word."

Gawain's brothers were Agrivain, Gahariet, and Gareth.

Sir Gawain's Marriage
Once upon a time King Arthur held his court in merry Carlisle, when a damsel came before him and craved a boon. It was for vengeance upon a caitiff knight, who had made her lover captive and despoiled her of her lands. King Arthur

commanded to bring him his sword, Excalibar, and to saddle his steed, and rode forth without delay to right the lady's wrong. Ere long he reached the castle of the grim baron, and challenged him to the conflict. But the castle stood on magic ground, and the spell was such that no knight could tread theron but straight his courage fell and his strength decayed. King Arthur felt the charm, and before a blow was struck, his sturdy limbs lost their strength, and his head grew faint. He was fain to yield himself prisoner to the churlish knight, who refused to release him except upon condition that he should return at the end of a year, and bring a true answer to the question, "What thing is it which women most desire?" or in default thereof surrender himself and his lands. King Arthur accepted the terms, and gave his oath to return at the time appointed. During the year the king rode east, and

he rode west, and inquired of all whom he met what thing it is which all women most desire. Some told him riches; some, pomp and state; some, mirth; some, flattery; and some, a gallant knight. But in the diversity of answers he could find no sure dependence. The year was well-nigh spent, when one day, as he rode thoughtfully through a forest, he saw sitting beneath a tree a lady of such hideous aspect that he turned away his eyes, and when she greeted him in seemly sort, made no answer. "What wight art thou," the lady said, "that will not speak to me? It may chance that I may resolve thy doubts, though I be not fair of aspect." "If thou wilt do so," said King Arthur, "choose what reward thou wilt,

thou grim lady, and it shall be given
thee." "Swear me this upon thy faith,"
she said, and Arthur swore it. Then the
lady told him the secret, and demanded
her reward, which was that the king
should find some fair and courtly knight
to be her husband.

King Arthur hastened to the grim
baron's castle and told him one by one all
the answers which he had received from
his various advisers, except the last, and
not one was admitted as the true one.
"Now yield thee, Arthur," the giant said,
"for thou hast not paid thy ransom, and
thou and thy lands are forfeited to me."
Then King Arthur said:

"Yet hold thy hand, thou proud baron,
　　I pray thee hold thy hand,
And give me leave to speak once more,
　　In rescue of my land.
This morn as I came over a moor,
　　I saw a lady set,

Between an oak and a green holly,
　　All clad in red scarlett.
She says *all women would have their will*,
　　This is their chief desire;
Now yield, as thou art a baron true,
　　That I have paid my hire.

"It was my sister that told thee this," the
churlish baron exclaimed. "Vengeance
light on her! I will some time or other do
her as ill a turn."

King Arthur rode homeward, but not
light of heart, for he remembered the
promise he was under to the loathly lady
to give her one of his young and gallant
knights for a husband. He told his grief
to Sir Gawain, his nephew, and he
replied, "Be not sad, my lord, for I will
marry the loathly lady." King Arthur
replied:

"Now nay, now nay, good Sir Gawaine,
　　My sister's son ye be;

The loathly lady's all too grim,
And all too foule for thee."

But Gawain persisted, and the king at last, with sorrow of heart, consented that Gawain should be his ransom. So one day the king and his knights rode to the forest, met the loathly lady, and brought her to the court. Sir Gawain stood the scoffs and jeers of his companions as he best might, and the marriage was solemnized, but not with the usual festivities. Chaucer tells us:

". . . There was no joye ne feste at alle;
There n' as but hevinesse and mochel
     sorwe,
For prively he wed her on the morwe,
And all day after hid him as an owle,
So wo was him his wife loked so foule!"

When night came, and they were alone together, Sir Gawain could not conceal his aversion; and the lady asked him why he sighed so heavily, and turned away his face. He candidly confessed it was on account of three things: her age, her ugliness, and her low degree. The lady, not at all offended, replied with excellent arguments to all his objections. She showed him that with age is discretion, with ugliness security from rivals, and that all true gentility depends, not upon the accident of birth, but upon the character of the individual.

Sir Gawain made no reply; but,

turning his eyes on his bride, what was his amazement to perceive that she wore no longer the unseemly aspect that had so distressed him. She then told him that the form she had worn was not her true form, but a disguise imposed upon her by a wicked enchanter, and that she was condemned to wear it until two things should happen: one, that she should obtain some young and gallant knight to be her husband. This having been done, one-half of the charm was removed. She was now at liberty to wear her true form for half the time, and she bade him choose whether he would have her fair by day, and ugly by night, or the reverse. Sir Gawain would fain have had her look her best by night, when he alone would see her, and show her repulsive visage, if at all, to others. But she reminded him how much more pleasant it would be to her to wear her best looks in the throng of knights and ladies by day. Sir Gawain

yielded, and gave up his will to hers. This alone was wanting to dissolve the charm. The lovely lady now with joy assured him that she should change no more, but as she now was, so would she remain by night as well as by day.

"Sweet blushes stayned her rud-red cheek,
    Her eyen were black as sloe,
The ripening cherrye swelled her lippe,
    And all her neck was snow.
Sir Gawain kist that ladye faire
    Lying upon the sheete,
And swore, as he was a true knight,
    The spice was never so swete."

The dissolution of the charm which had held the lady also released her brother, the "grim baron," for he too had been implicated in it. He ceased to be a churlish oppressor, and became a gallant and generous knight as any at Arthur's court.

somewhere i have never travelled
e. e. cummings

somewhere i have never travelled, gladly beyond
any experience, your eyes have their silence:
in your most frail gesture are things which enclose me,
or which i cannot touch because they are too near

your slightest look easily will unclose me
though i have closed myself as fingers,
you open always petal by petal myself as Spring opens
(touching skillfully, mysteriously) her first rose

or if your wish be to close me, i and
my life will shut very beautifully, suddenly,
as when the heart of this flower imagines
the snow carefully everywhere descending;

nothing which we are to perceive in this world equals
the power of your intense fragility: whose texture
compels me with the colour of its countries,
rendering death and forever with each breathing

(i do not know what it is about you that closes
and opens; only something in me understands
the voice of your eyes is deeper than all roses)
nobody, not even the rain, has such small hands

Fortune Cookies

*L*ike love, these cookies must be made gently, sensitively, and with confidence. Wear light cotton gloves if your hands are sensitive to heat and remember, the cookies are only pliable when they are hot. The fortunes can be put in before you fold, or after. The traditional size for the fortune is $1/2$ x 3 inches.

1 cup all-purpose white flour
$1/2$ teaspoon salt
2 tablespoons cornstarch
$1/3$ cup sugar
$1/2$ cup vegetable oil
$1/3$ cup egg whites
$1/3$ cup water

1. Preheat the oven to 300°F and line cookie sheets with aluminum foil. Butter the foil.
2. Sift together all the dry ingredients. Add the oil and the egg whites and stir until smooth. Add the water and stir until blended.
3. Start by baking just a few cookies. Drop one tablespoon of batter at a time onto the cookie sheet several inches apart. With the back of the spoon, smooth cookies into 4-inch circles. Bake cookies for approximately 10 minutes until they begin to brown.
4. With a wide spatula, remove cookies from the oven one at a time. Flip each one upside down onto your hand, lay the fortune down on top of it, and fold cookie in half. Then fold that semicircle in half by bending it over the edge of the pan so that it is creased down the middle but the two sides do not touch.
5. Set in an empty egg carton. When cool, store in an airtight container.

SOME IDEAS FOR FORTUNES:
• Yes • No • Maybe • When?
• Tonight • Birds do it, bees do it, you, too, will do it • Good for more than one movie (kiss . . .) • It's very simple. Her (his) love is here to stay • Marry me? • Soon you will move in with the man of your dreams • Rainbows will surround you • Soon white powdered sand will lie beneath your feet • Delicious things will happen to you • You will leave for Hawaii on September 7th with the man you love

from the Journal of . . .
Charles Darwin

This is the Question

Marry

Children—(if it please God)—constant
companion, (friend in old age) who will feel
interested in one, object to be beloved and
played with—better than a dog anyhow—
Home, and someone to take care of house—
Charms of music and female chit-chat. These
things good for one's health. Forced to visit
and receive relations but terrible loss of time.

My God, it is intolerable to think of
spending one's whole life, like a neuter bee,

66

working, working and nothing after all.
—No, no won't do—
 Imagine living all one's day solitarily in
smoky dirty London House.—Only picture to
yourself a nice soft wife on a sofa with good
fire, and books and music perhaps—compare
this vision with the dingy reality of Grt.
Marlboro' St. Marry—Marry—Marry Q.E.D.

Not Marry

No children, (no second life) no one to care for
one in old age.—What is the use of working
without sympathy from near and dear
friends—who are near and dear friends to
the old except relatives.

67

from the Journal of . . . Charles Darwin

Freedom to go where one liked—Choice of Society and little of it. Conversation of clever men at clubs.—

Not forced to visit relatives, and to bend in every trifle—to have the expense and anxiety of children—perhaps quarrelling.

Loss of time—cannot read in the evenings—fatness and idleness—anxiety and responsibility—less money for books etc.—if many children forced to gain one's bread.—(But then it is very bad for one's health to work too much)

Perhaps my wife won't like London; then the sentence is banishment and degradation with indolent idle fool—

On the reverse side he wrote:

It being proved necessary to marry—When? Soon or Late. The Governor says soon for otherwise had if one has children—one's character is more flexible—one's feelings more lively, and if one does not marry soon, one misses so much good pure happiness.—

But then if I married tomorrow. there would be an infinity of trouble and expense in getting and furnishing a house,—fighting about no Society—morning calls—awkwardness—loss of time every day—(without one's wife was an angel and made one keep industrious)—Then how should I manage all my business if I were obliged to go every day walking with my

70

wife.—Eheu!! I never should know French,—or
see the Continent,—or go to America, or go up
in a Balloon, or take solitary trip in Wales—
poor slave, you will be worse than a negro—
And then horrid poverty (without one's wife
was better than an angel and had money)—
Never mind my boy—Cheer up—One cannot
live this solitary life, with groggy old age,
friendless and cold and childless staring one
in one's face, already beginning to wrinkle.
Never mind, trust to chance—keep a sharp look
out.—There is many a happy slave—

Celebrated naturalist Charles Darwin married
Emma Wedgwood on January 29, 1839.
Their lives together ended with his death in 1882.

The Rainbow

D. H. Lawrence

"I came up," he said, speaking curiously matter-of-fact and level, "to ask if you'd marry me. You are free, aren't you?"

There was a long silence, whilst his blue eyes, strangely impersonal, looked into her eyes to seek an answer to the truth. He was looking for the truth out of her. And she, as if hypnotized, must answer at length.

"Yes, I am free to marry."

The expression of his eyes changed, became less impersonal, as if he were looking almost at her, for the truth of her. Steady and intent and eternal they were, as if they would never change. They seemed to fix and to resolve her. She quivered, feeling herself created, will-less, lapsing into him, into a common will with him.

"You want me?" she said.

A pallor came over his face.

"Yes," he said.

Still there was suspense and silence.

"No," she said, not of herself. "No, I don't know."

He felt the tension breaking up in him, his fists slackened, he was unable to move. He stood looking at her, helpless in his vague collapse. For the moment she had become unreal to him. Then he saw her come to him, curiously direct and as if without movement, in a sudden flow. She put her hand to his coat.

"Yes I want to," she said impersonally, looking at him with wide, candid, newly-opened eyes, opened now with supreme truth. He went very white as he stood, and did not move, only his eyes were held by hers, and he suffered. She seemed to see him with her newly-opened, wide eyes, almost of a child, and with a strange movement, that was agony to him, she reached slowly forward her dark face and her breast to him, with a slow insinuation of a kiss that made something

break in his brain, and it was darkness over him for a few moments.

He had her in his arms, and, obliterated, was kissing her. And it was sheer, blenched agony to him, to break away from himself. She was there so small and light and accepting in his arms, like a child, and yet with such an insinuation of embrace, of infinite embrace, that he could not bear it, he could not stand.

He turned and looked for a chair, and keeping her still in his arms, sat down with her close to him, to his breast. Then, for a few seconds, he went utterly to sleep, asleep and sealed in the darkest sleep, utter, extreme oblivion.

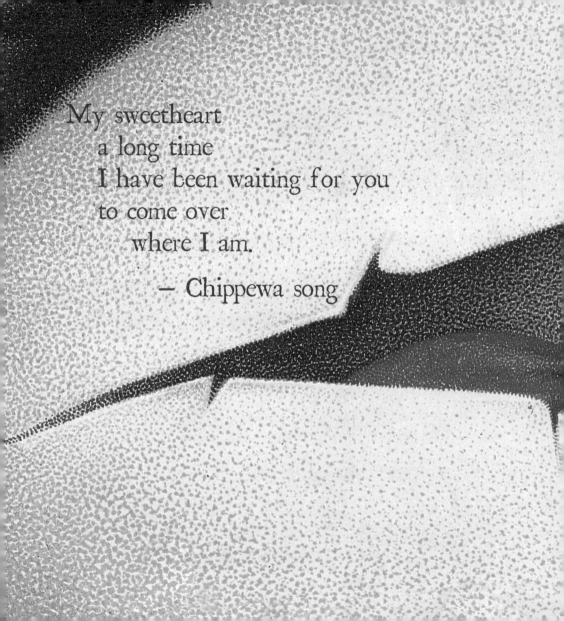

My sweetheart
  a long time
I have been waiting for you
to come over
    where I am.

    — Chippewa song

Love One Another
Kahlil Gibran

Love one another, but make not a bond of love:
Let it rather be a moving sea between the
    shores of your souls.
Fill each other's cup but drink not from one cup.
Give one another of your bread but eat not from
    the same loaf.
Sing and dance together and be joyous, but let
    each one of you be alone,
Even as the strings of a lute are alone though
    they quiver with the same music.
Give your hearts, but not into each other's keeping.
For only the hand of Life can contain your hearts.
And stand together yet not too near together:
For the pillars of the temple stand apart,
And the oak tree and the cypress grow not
    in each other's shadow.

Letter from Simon Fallowfield to Mary Foster

My Dear Miss,   **November 29th, 1866**

I now take up my pen to write to you hoping these few lines will find you well as it leaves me at present Thank God for it. You will perhaps be surprised that I should make so bold as to write to you who is such a lady and I hope you will not be vex at me for it. I hardly dare say what I want, I am so timid about ladies, and my heart trimmels like a hespin. But I once seed in a book that faint heart never won fair lady, so here goes.

I am a farmer in a small way and my age is rather more than forty years and my mother lives with me and keeps my house, and she has been very poorly lately and cannot stir about much and I think I should be more comfortabler with a wife.

I have had my eye on you a long time and I think you are a very nice young woman and one that would make me

Simon Fallowfield to Mary Foster

happy if only you think so. We keep a servant girl to milk three kye and do the work in the house, and she goes out a bit in the summer to gadder wickens and she snags a few of turnips in the back kend. I do a piece of work on the farm myself and attends Pately Market, and I sometimes show a few sheep and I feeds between 3 & 4 pigs agen Christmas, and the same is very useful in the house to make pies and cakes and so forth, and I sells the hams to help pay for the barley meal.

I have about 73 pund in Naisbro Bank and we have a nice little parlour downstairs with a blue carpet, and an oven on the side of the fireplace and the old woman on the other side smoking. The Golden Rules claimed up on the walls above the long settle, and you could sit all day in the easy chair and knit and mend my kytles and leggums, and you could make the tea ready agin I come in, and you could make butter for Pately Market, and I would drive you to church every Sunday in the spring cart, and I would do all that bees in my power to make you happy. So I hope to hear from you. I am

Simon Fallowfield to Mary Foster

in desprit and Yurnest, and will marry you at May Day, or if my mother dies afore I shall want you afore. If only you will accept of me, my dear, we could be very happy together.

I hope you will let me know your mind by return of post, and if you are favourable I will come up to scratch. So no more at present from your well-wisher and true love—

Simon Fallowfield

P.S. I hope you will say nothing about this. If you will not accept of me I have another very nice woman in my eye, and I think I shall marry her if you do not accept of me, but I thought you would suit me mother better, she being very crusty at times. So I tell you now before you come, she will be Maister.

Simon Fallowfield, an uneducated young farmer, proposed to Mary Foster, a young lady from the village of Middlemoor Pately Bridge in Yorkshire, through an advertisement. She refused.

Night & Day

Cole Porter

Like the beat, beat, beat
   of the tom-tom
When the jungle shadows fall,
Like the tick, tick, tock of the
   stately clock
As it stands against the wall,
Like the drip, drip, drip,
   of the raindrops,
When the summer show'r is through,
So a voice within me keeps repeating,
You, you, you.

Night and day you are the one,
Only you beneath the moon and
   under the sun,
Whether near to me or far,
It's no matter, darling, where you are,
I think of you, night and day.

Day and night why is it so,
That this longing for you follows
   wherever I go?
In the roaring traffic's boom,
In the silence of my lonely room,
I think of you, night and day.

Night and day under the hide of me,
There's an, oh, such a hungry
   yearning, burning inside of me.
And its torment won't be through
'Til you let me spend my life
   making love to you
Day and night,
   night and day.

The Owl and the Pussy-Cat
Edward Lear

The Owl and the Pussy-Cat went to sea
    In a beautiful pea-green boat.
They took some honey, and plenty of money
    Wrapped up in a five-pound note.
The Owl looked up to the stars above,
    And sang to a small guitar,
"O lovely Pussy! O pussy, my love,
What a beautiful Pussy you are,
            You are,
            You are!
What a beautiful Pussy you are!"

Pussy said to the Owl, "You elegant fowl!
    How charmingly sweet you sing!
O let us be married! too long we have tarried:
    But what shall we do for a ring?"
They sailed away, for a year and a day,
    To the land where the Bong-Tree grows,

And there in a wood a Piggy-wig stood,
With a ring at the end of his nose,
His nose,
His nose!
With a ring at the end of his nose.

"Dear Pig, are you willing to sell for one shilling
Your ring?" Said the Piggy, "I will."
So they took it away, and were married next day
By the Turkey who lives on the hill.
They dined on mince, and slices of quince,
Which they ate with a runcible spoon;
And hand in hand, on the edge of the sand
They danced by the light of the moon,
The moon,
The moon,
They danced by the light of the moon.

The Velveteen Rabbit

Margery Williams

"What is REAL?" asked the Rabbit one day, when they were lying side by side near the nursery fender, before Nana came to tidy the room. "Does it mean having things that buzz inside you and a stick-out handle?"

"Real isn't how you are made," said the Skin Horse. "It's a thing that happens to you. When a child loves you for a long, long time, not just to play with, but *really* loves you, then you become Real."

"Does it hurt?" asked the Rabbit.

"Sometimes," said the Skin Horse, for he was always truthful. "When you are Real you don't mind being hurt."

"Does it happen all at once, like being wound up," he asked, "or bit by bit?"

"It doesn't happen all at once," said the Skin Horse. "You become. It takes a long time. That's why it doesn't often happen to people who break easily, or have sharp edges, or who have to be carefully kept. Generally, by the time you are Real, most of your hair has been loved off, and your eyes drop out and you get loose in the joints and very shabby. But these things don't matter at all, because once you are Real, you can't be ugly except to people who don't understand."

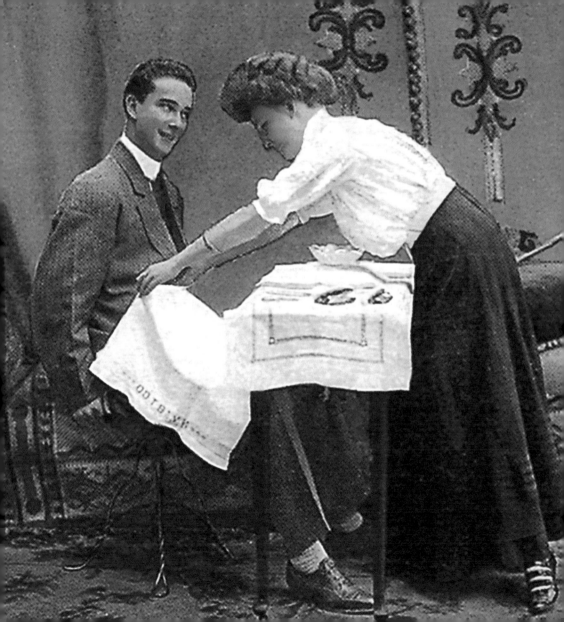

The Aphrodisiac Dinner for Him

This dinner is made early in the day so the cook can be with her man all evening. The chicken is baked wrapped in ti leaves, imported from Hawaii, which you will need to order in advance from a flower shop. If you absolutely cannot find Hawaiian salt, use coarse sea salt as a substitute.

Honeymoon Chicken
(aka Laulau)

4 tablespoons butter
1 lemon, cut into quarters
1 sweet onion, cut into quarters
2 teaspoons Hawaiian salt
1 3^1/2 lb. chicken
1^1/2 cups cooked white rice
6 ti leaves

1. Put half the butter, lemon, onion, and salt into the cavity of the chicken. Add the rice, then the remaining butter, lemon, and onion.
2. Sprinkle the outside of the chicken with remaining salt.
3. On a piece of aluminum foil large enough to wrap the chicken, arrange the ti leaves—cut stems in the center, radiating out like a sunburst.
4. Place the chicken on the leaves and wrap them around the chicken.
5. Wrap with foil, covering lightly.
6. Bake in a shallow roasting pan at 350°F for 3 hours.

Artichokes with Lime Butter

2 large artichokes
^{1}/2 cup butter, melted
juice of ^{1}/2 lime

1. Steam 2 artichokes, stems up, in a covered pot for 30–40 minutes, depending on their size.

The Aphrodisiac Dinner for Him (continued)

2. Test for doneness by piercing the stems with a fork; they will give easily.
3. Serve with 1/2 cup melted butter, with juice of 1/2 lime added.

Seduction Salad

1 15-oz. can black beans
1 avocado
1 papaya
2 teaspoons Hawaiian salt
2 tablespoons cilantro leaves, finely chopped
2 teaspoons cracked pepper
1 tablespoon fresh lime juice
2 shallots, finely chopped
1 8-oz. can crushed pineapple in its own juice

1. Divide the black beans and arrange on each of two salad plates.
2. Peel and cut slices of avocado and papaya, placing 1/2 of each fruit on the beans in each plate.
3. Crush salt, cilantro leaves, and pepper in a small bowl with the back of a spoon.
4. Add lime juice, shallots, and pineapple; mix. Spoon over the beans and fruit.

Honey Figs

1 tablespoon honey
6 figs, cut in half lengthwise
3 oz. whipping cream
1/2 teaspoon vanilla
1 teaspoon honey

1. Melt 1 tablespoon honey in a small heavy-bottom pan.
2. Place figs cut-side down on the hot honey.
3. Cook, shaking the pan often, until honey begins to caramelize (bubble and brown).
4. Whip the cream; add vanilla and 1 teaspoon honey.
5. Serve the figs cut-side up, topped with whipped cream and Cookie Valentines.

Cookie Valentines

12 tablespoons unsalted butter, at room temperature
1/2 cup sugar
grated zest from 2 oranges
3/4 teaspoon salt
1 egg
1/2 teaspoon pure vanilla extract
2 cups unbleached white flour

1. With electric mixer at medium speed, beat butter, sugar, orange zest, and salt until creamy. Add egg and vanilla and continue beating until light and fluffy. With a spoon, gradually beat in the flour. Divide dough in half; shape each section into a disc and wrap in plastic wrap. Chill until firm enough to roll, approximately 1 hour.
2. Heat oven to 325°F.
3. Roll out dough between 2 pieces of plastic wrap to about 1/4-inch thickness. Cut dough with a 3-inch heart cookie cutter.
4. Place cookies approximately 1 inch apart on ungreased cookie sheets. Bake until edges just begin to brown, about 15 minutes.
5. Remove to racks and cool completely.

*Letters between John Middleton Murry
and his wife, Katherine Mansfield*

TO KATHERINE   14 January 1918

. . . As I got up from my chair, I saw your letter lying on
the little round table in front of me. I had to kiss it: then
I stood by the fire and looked at the clock, and loved you
so much that I thought my heart would burst. I wondered whether
some thing would tell you that I was full of love of you, wanting
you to know I loved you so deeply, at a quarter to twelve on
Monday night. Then I got down your photograph. It's stuck in a
corner of the looking glass. And I was knocked all of a heap by
your beauty again. It's the photo where you have the black jacket on,
and the marguerite on your button-hole. And there is all that
wonderful, secret child-ness, trembling about that impossibly delicate
mouth. You darling, darling, darling. That's only the first words of
what I said to you. You exquisite, incredible woman.

John Middleton Murry and Katherine Mansfield

TO JOHN   *27 January 1918*

My love for you tonight is so deep and tender that it seems to be outside myself as well. I am fast shut up like a little lake in the embrace of some big mountains. If you were to climb up the mountains, you would see me down below, deep and shining—and quite fathomless, my dear. You might drop your heart into me and you'd never hear it touch bottom. I love you—I love you— Goodnight. Oh, Bogey, what it is to love like this!

Katherine Mansfield, New Zealand-born British writer, married John Middleton Murry, English writer and critic, in 1918. They were together until her death in 1923.

96

Love's Philosophy
Percy Bysshe Shelley

The fountains mingle with the river
    And the rivers with the Ocean,
The winds of Heaven mix for ever
    With a sweet emotion;
Nothing in the world is single;
    All things by a law divine
In one spirit meet and mingle,
    Why not I with thine?—

See the mountains kiss high Heaven
    And the waves clasp one another;
No sister-flower would be forgiven
    If it disdained its brother;
And the sunlight clasps the earth
    And the moonbeams kiss the sea:
What is all this sweet work worth
    If thou kiss not me?

Henry V

William Shakespeare

KING HENRY. Fair Katharine, and most fair,
Will you vouchsafe to teach a soldier terms
Such as will enter at a lady's ear
And plead his love-suit to her gentle heart?

KATHARINE. Your majesty shall mock at me; I cannot speak your
England.

KING HENRY. O fair Katharine, if you will love me soundly with your
French heart, I will be glad to hear you confess it
brokenly with your English tongue. Do you like me, Kate?

KATHARINE. Pardonnez-moi, I cannot tell vat is "like me."

KING HENRY. An angel is like you, Kate, and you are like an angel.

KATHARINE. Que dit-il? que je suis semblable a les anges?

ALICE. Oui, vraiment, sauf votre grace, ainsi dit-il.

KING HENRY. I said so, dear Katharine, and I must not blush to affirm it.

100

KATHARINE.   O bon Dieu! les langues des hommes sont pleines de tromperies.

KING HENRY.   What says she, fair one? that the tongues of men are full of deceits?

ALICE.   Oui, dat de tongues of de mans is be full of deceits: dat is de princess.

KING HENRY.   The princess is the better Englishwoman. I' faith, Kate, my wooing is fit for thy understanding; I am glad thou canst speak no better English; for if thou couldst, thou wouldst find me such a plain king that thou wouldst think I had sold my farm to buy my crown. I know no ways to mince it in love, but directly to say, "I love you": then if you urge me farther than to say, "Do you in faith?" I wear out my suit. Give me your answer; i' faith, do: and so clap hands and a bargain: How say you, lady?

KATHARINE.   Sauf votre honneur, me understand well.

KING HENRY.   Marry, if you would put me to verses, or to dance for your sake, Kate, why you undid me: for the one, I have neither words nor measure, and for the other, I have no strength in measure, yet a reasonable measure in strength. If I could win a lady at leap-frog, or by vaulting into my saddle with my armour on my back, under the correction of bragging be it spoken, I should quickly leap into a wife.

Or if I might buffet for my love, or bound my horse for
her favours, I could lay on like a butcher and sit like a
jack-an-apes, never off. But, before God, Kate, I cannot
look greenly nor gasp out my eloquence, nor I have no
cunning in protestation; only downright oaths, which I
never use till urged, nor never break for urging. If thou
canst love a fellow of this temper, Kate, whose face is not
worth sun-burning, that never looks in his glass for love of
any thing he sees there, let thine eye be thy cook. I speak
to thee plain soldier: if thou canst love me for this, take
me; if not, to say to thee that I shall die, is true; but for
thy love, by the Lord, no; yet I love thee too. And while
thou livest, dear Kate, take a fellow of plain and uncoined
constancy; for he perforce must do thee right, because he
hath not the gift to woo in other places: for these fellows
of infinite tongue, that can rhyme themselves into ladies'
favours, they do always reason themselves out again.
What! a speaker is but a prater; a rhyme is but a ballad.
A good leg will fall, a straight back will stoop, a black
beard will turn white, a curled pate will grow bald, a fair
face will wither, a full eye will wax hollow, but a good
heart, Kate, is the sun and the moon; or rather the sun,
and not the moon; for it shines bright and never changes,

but keeps his course truly. If thou would have such a one, take me; and take me, take a soldier; take a soldier, take a king. And what sayest thou then to my love? speak, my fair, and fairly, I pray thee.

KATHARINE.   Is it possible dat I sould love de enemy of France?

KING HENRY.   No; it is not possible you should love the enemy of France, Kate; but, in loving me, you should love the friend of France; for I love France so well that I will not part with a village of it; I will have it all mine: and Kate, when France is mine and I am yours, then yours is France and you are mine.

KATHARINE.   I cannot tell wat is dat.

KING HENRY.   No, Kate? I will tell thee in French, which I am sure will hang upon my tongue like a new-married wife about her husband's neck, hardly to be shook off. Je quand sur le possession de France, et quand vous avez le possession de moi,—let me see, what then? Saint Denis be my speed!— donc votre est France et vous êtes mienne. It is as easy for me, Kate, to conquer the kingdom as to speak so much more French: I shall never move thee in French, unless it be to laugh at me.

KATHARINE.   Sauf votre honneur, le Français que vous parlez, il est meilleur que l'Anglais lequel je parle.

KING HENRY. No, faith, is't not, Kate; but thy speaking of my tongue, and I thine, most truly-falsely, must needs be granted to be much at one. But, Kate, dost thou understand thus much English? Canst thou love me?

KATHARINE. I cannot tell.

~

KING HENRY. Come, your answer in broken music; for thy voice is music and thy English broken; therefore, queen of all, Katharine, break thy mind to me in broken English: wilt thou have me?

KATHARINE. Dat is as it shall please de roi mon père.

KING HENRY. Nay, it will please him well, Kate; it shall please him, Kate.

KATHARINE. Den it sall also content me.

KING HENRY. Upon that I kiss your hand, and I call you my queen.

KATHARINE. Laissez, mon seigneur, laissez, laissez! Ma foi, je ne veux point que vous abaissiez votre grandeur en baisant la main d'une de votre seigneurie indigne serviteur; excusez-moi, je vous supplie, mon très puissant seigneur.

KING HENRY. Then I will kiss your lips, Kate.

KATHARINE. Les dames et demoiselles, pour être baisées devant leur noces, il n'est pas la coutume de France.

KING HENRY. Madam my interpreter, what says she?

ALICE: Dat it is not be de fashion pour les ladies of France,—I
             cannot tell vat is baiser en Anglish.

KING HENRY. To kiss.

ALICE.   Your majesty entendre better que moi.

KING HENRY. It is not a fashion for the maids in France to kiss before
             they are married, would she say?

ALICE.   Oui, vraiment.

KING HENRY. O Kate! nice customs curtsy to great kings. Dear Kate,
             you and I cannot be confined within the weak list of a
             country's fashion: we are the makers of manners, Kate;
             and the liberty that follows our places stops the mouth of
             all find-faults; as I will do yours, for upholding the nice
             fashion of your country in denying me a kiss: therefore,
             patiently and yielding.

Kissing her. You have witchcraft in your lips, Kate: there is more
             eloquence in a sugar touch of them than in the tongues of
             the French council; and they should sooner persuade
             Harry of England than a general petition of monarchs.
             Here comes your father.

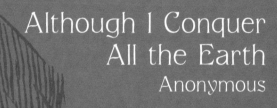

Although I Conquer
All the Earth
Anonymous

Although I conquer all the earth,
Yet for me there is only one city.
In that city there is for me only one house;
And in that house, one room only;
And in that room, a bed.
And one woman sleeps there,
The shining joy and jewel of all my kingdom.

Letters between Winston Churchill and his wife, Clementine

TO WINSTON   *November 28, 1915*

... But when I think of you my Dearest Darling, I forget all disappointment, bitterness or ambition & long to have you safe & warm & alive in my arms. Since you have re-become a soldier I look upon civilians of high or low degree with pity & indulgence— The wives of men over military age may be lucky but I am sorry for them being married to feeble & incompetent old men.

I think you will get this letter on your birthday & it brings you all my love & many passionate kisses— My Darling Darling Winston—I find my morning breakfast lonely without you, so Sarah fills your place & does her best to look almost exactly like you. I'm keeping the flag flying till you return by getting up early & having breakfast down-stairs.

Winston and Clementine Churchill

TO CLEMENTINE   *December 1, 1915*

I reopen my envelope to tell you I have recd your dear letter of the 28th. I reciprocate intensely the feelings of love & devotion you show to me. My greatest good fortune in a life of brilliant experience has been to find you, & to lead my life with you. I don't feel far away from you out here at all. I feel vy near in my heart; & also I feel that the nearer I get to honour, the nearer I am to you.

Winston Churchill, British prime minister and author, wed Clementine Hozier in 1908. They were happily married for 57 years.

My most brilliant achievement was my ability to be able to persuade my wife to marry me.

– Winston Churchill

The Elephant & The Butterfly

e. e. cummings

Once upon a time there was an elephant who did nothing all day.

He lived by himself in a little house away at the very top of a curling road.

From the elephant's house, this curling road went twisting away down and down until it found itself in a green valley where there was another little house, in which a butterfly lived.

One day the elephant was sitting in his little house and looking out of his window doing nothing (and feeling very happy because that was what he liked most to do) when along this curling road he saw somebody coming up and up toward his little house; and he opened his eyes wide, and felt very much surprised. "Whoever is that person who's coming up along and along the curling road toward my little house?" the elephant said to himself.

And pretty soon he saw that it was a butterfly who was fluttering along the curling road ever so happily; and the elephant said: "My

116

goodness, I wonder if he's coming to call on me?" As the butterfly came nearer and nearer, the elephant felt more and more excited inside of himself. Up the steps of the little house came the butterfly and he knocked very gently on the door with his wing. "Is anyone inside?" he asked.

The elephant was ever so pleased, but he waited.

Then the butterfly knocked again with his wing, a little louder but still very gently, and said: "Does anyone live here, please?"

Still the elephant never said anything because he was too happy to speak.

A third time the butterfly knocked, this time quite loudly, and asked: "Is anyone at home?" And this time the elephant said in a trembling voice: "I am." The butterfly peeped in at the door

and said: "Who are you, that live in this little house?" And the elephant peeped out at him and answered: "I'm the elephant who does nothing all day."

"Oh," said the butterfly, "and may I come in?"

"Please do," the elephant said with a smile, because he was very happy. So the butterfly just pushed the little door open with his wing and came in.

Once upon a time there were seven trees which lived beside the curling road. And when the butterfly pushed the door with his wing and came into the elephant's little house, one of the trees said to one of the trees: "I think it's going to rain soon."

"The curling road will be all wet and will smell beautifully," said another tree to another tree.

Then a different tree said to a different tree: "How lucky for the

117

butterfly that he's safely inside the elephant's little house, because he won't mind the rain."

But the littlest tree said: "I feel the rain already," and sure enough, while the butterfly and the elephant were talking in the elephant's little house away at the top of the curling road, the rain simply began falling gently everywhere; and the butterfly and the elephant looked out of the window together and they felt ever so safe and glad, while the curling road became all wet and began to smell beautifully just as the third tree had said.

Pretty soon it stopped raining and the elephant put his arm very gently around the little butterfly and said: "Do you love me a little?"

And the butterfly smiled and said: "No, I love you very much."

Then the elephant said: "I'm so happy, I think we ought to go for a walk

together you and I; for now the rain has stopped and the curling road smells beautifully."

The butterfly sail: "Yes, but where shall you and I go?"

"Let's go away down and down the curling road where I've never been," the elephant said to the little butterfly. And the butterfly smiled and said: "I'd love to go with you away and away down the curling road—let's go out the little door of your house and down the steps together—shall we?"

So they came out together and the elephant's arm was very gently around the butterfly. Then the littlest tree said to his six friends: "I believe the butterfly loves the elephant as much as the elephant loves the butterfly, and that makes me very happy, for they'll love each other always."

Down and down the curling road walked the elephant and the butterfly.

The sun was shining beautifully after the rain.

The curling road smelled beautifully of flowers.

A bird began to sing in a bush, and all the clouds went away out of the sky and it was Spring everywhere.

When they came to the butterfly's house, which was down in the green valley which had never been so green, the elephant said: "Is this where you live?"

And the butterfly said: "Yes, this is where I live."

"May I come into your house?" Said the elephant.

"Yes," said the butterfly. So the elephant just pushed the door gently with his trunk and they came into the butterfly's house. And then the elephant kissed the butterfly very gently and the butterfly said: "Why didn't you ever before come down into the valley where I live?" And the elephant answered, "Because I did nothing all day. But now that I know where you live, I'm coming down the curling road to see you every day, if I may—and may I come?" Then the butterfly kissed the elephant and said: "I love you, so please do."

And every day after this the elephant would come down the curling road which smelled so beautifully (past the seven trees and the bird singing in the bush) to visit his little friend the butterfly.

And they loved each other always.

I've Got You Under My Skin

Cole Porter

I've got you under my skin,
I've got you deep in the heart of me,
So deep in my heart, you're really a part of me.
I've got you under my skin.

I tried so not to give in,
I said to myself, "This affair never will go so well?"
But why should I try to resist when, darling, I know so well
I've got you under my skin.
I'd sacrifice anything, come what might,
For the sake of having you near,
In spite of a warning voice that comes in the night,
And repeats and repeats in my ear;
"Don't you know, little fool, you never can win,
Use your mentality,
Wake up to reality."
But each time I do, just the thought of you
Makes me stop, before I begin,
'Cause I've got you under my skin.

Love Song
William Carlos Williams

Sweep the house clean,
hang fresh curtains
in the windows
put on a new dress
and come with me!
The elm is scattering
its little loaves
of sweet smells
from a white sky!
Who shall hear of us
in the time to come?
Let him say there was
a burst of fragrance
from black branches.

DEAR SIR,

Last Friday, Mr. Town, was Valentine's day; and I'll tell you what I did the night before. I got five bay-leaves, and pinned four of them to the four corners of my pillow, and the fifth to the middle; and then, if I dreamed of my sweetheart, Betty said we should be married before the year was out. But, to make it more sure, I boiled an egg hard, and took out the yolk, and filled it up with salt: and when I went to bed, eat it shell and all, without speaking or drinking after it, and this was to have the same effect with the bay-leaves. We also wrote our lovers' names upon bits of paper, and rolled them up in clay, and put them in water; and the first that rose up was to be our Valentine. Would you think it? Mr. Blossom was my man.

Dear Mr. Town, if you know any other ways to try our fortune by, do put them in your paper. My mama laughs at us, and says there is nothing in them; but I am sure there is, for several misses at our boarding-school have tried them, and they have all happened true.

Your humble servant,
Arabella Whimsey

She Walks in Beauty

Lord Byron

She walks in beauty, like the night
    Of cloudless climes and starry skies;
And all that's best of dark and bright
    Meet in her aspect and her eyes:
Thus mellowed to that tender light
    Which heaven to gaudy day denies.

One shade the more, one ray the less,
    Had half impaired the nameless grace
Which waves in every raven tress,
    Or softly lightens o'er her face;
Where thoughts serenely sweet express
    How pure, how dear their dwelling place.

And on that cheek, and o'er that brow,
    So soft, so calm, yet eloquent,
The smiles that win, the tints that glow,
    But tell of days in goodness spent,
A mind at peace with all below,
    A heart whose love is innocent!

Sinful Chocolate Fondue

(Serves two extremely enthusiastic participants)

Gather assorted fruits (strawberries, bananas, apricots, pears, etc.) and/or assorted cakes and cookies (pound cake, brownies, ginger cookies, etc.).

FRUIT

1. Line a baking sheet with parchment paper. On wooden skewers, place desired pieces of fruit or cake, taking care to wash fruit and check for any blemishes, mold, etc.
2. Place skewers in freezer one hour prior to serving.

CHOCOLATE SAUCE

8 oz. semi-sweet or bittersweet chocolate
1/2 cup sweetened condensed milk
2 tablespoons unsalted butter
2 tablespoons orange juice
1/4 cup heavy whipping cream

1. Melt all ingredients in a double boiler, stirring constantly.
2. Place in a serving bowl and allow to cool slightly before serving.
3. Serve with assorted fruits and cakes, stirring occasionally.
4. If chocolate begins to harden, place in microwave for 5-second intervals, stirring until desired consistency is reached (or serve in fondue pot with lighted candle underneath to keep chocolate warm).

Jane Eyre

Charlotte Brontë

The house presented two pointed gables in its front: the windows were latticed and narrow: the front-door was narrow too, one step led up to it. The whole looked, as the host of Rochester Arms had said, "quite a desolate spot." It was as still as a church on a weekday: the pattering rain on the forest leaves was the only sound audible in its vicinage.

"Can there be life here?" I asked.

Yes: life of some kind there was; for I heard a movement—that narrow front-door was unclosing, and some shape was about to issue from the grange.

It opened slowly; a figure came out into the twilight and stood on the step; a man without a hat: he stretched forth his hand as if to feel whether it rained. Dusk as it was, I had recognized him—it was my master, Edward Fairfax Rochester, and no other.

I stayed my step, almost my breath, and stood to watch him—to examine him, myself unseen, and alas! to him invisible. It was a sudden meeting, and one in which rapture was kept well in check by pain. I had no difficulty in restraining my voice from exclamation, my step from hasty advance.

His form was of the same strong and stalwart contour as ever: his port was still erect, his hair was still raven-black; nor were his features altered or sunk: not in one year's space, by any sorrow, could his athletic strength be quelled, or his vigorous prime blighted. But in his countenance, I saw a change: that looked desperate and brooding—that reminded me of some wronged and fettered wild beast or bird, dangerous to approach in his sullen woe. The caged eagle, whose gold-ringed eyes cruelty has extinguished, might look as looked that sightless Samson.

And, reader, you think I feared him in his blind ferocity?—if you do, you little know me. A soft hope blent with my sorrow that soon I should dare to drop a kiss on that brow of rock, and on those lips so sternly sealed beneath it: but not yet. I would not accost him yet.

He descended the one step, and advanced slowly and gropingly towards the grass-plat. Where was his daring stride now? Then he paused, as if he knew not which way to turn. He lifted his hand and opened his eyelids; gazed blank, and with a straining effort, on the sky, and towards the amphitheatre of trees: one saw that all to him was void darkness. He stretched his right hand (the left arm, the mutilated one, he kept hidden in his bosom); he seemed to wish by touch to gain an idea of what lay around him: he met but vacancy still; for the trees were some yards off where he stood. he relinquished

133

the endeavour, folded his arms, and stood quiet and mute in the rain, now falling fast on his uncovered head. At this moment John approached him from some quarter.

"Will you take my arm, sir?" he said; "there is a heavy shower coming on: had you not better go in?"

"Let me alone," was the answer.

John withdrew, without having observed me. Mr. Rochester now tried to walk about: vainly,—all was too uncertain. He groped his way back to the house, and, re-entering it, closed the door.

I now drew near and knocked: John's wife opened for me. "Mary," I said, "how are you?"

She started as if she had seen a ghost: I calmed her. To her hurried "Is it really you, Miss, come at this late hour to this 'only place?" I answered by taking her hand; and then I followed her into the kitchen, where John now sat by a good

fire. I explained to them, in a few words, that I had heard all which had happened since I left Thornfield and that I was come to see Mr. Rochester. I asked John to go down to the turnpike-house, where I had dismissed the chaise, and bring my trunk, which I had left there: and then, while I removed my bonnet and shawl, I questioned Mary as to whether I could be accommodated at the Manor House for the night; and finding that arrangements to that effect, though difficult, would not be impossible, I informed her I should stay. Just at this moment the parlour-bell rang.

"When you go in," said I, "tell your master that a person wishes to speak to him, but do not give my name."

"I don't think he will see you," she answered; "he refuses everybody."

When she returned, I inquired what he had said.

"You are to send in your name and

your business," she replied. She then proceeded to fill a glass with water, and place it on a tray, together with candles.

"Is that what he rang for?" I asked.

"Yes: he always has candles brought in at dark, though he is blind."

"Give the tray to me, I will carry it in."

I took it from her hand: she pointed me out the parlour door. The tray shook as I held it; the water spilt from the glass; my heart struck my ribs loud and fast. Mary opened the door for me, and shut it behind me.

This parlour looked gloomy: a neglected handful of fire burnt low in the grate; and, leaning over it, with his head supported against the high, old-fashioned mantel-piece, appeared the blind tenant of the room. His old dog, Pilot, lay on one side, removed out of the way, and coiled up as if afraid of being inadvertently trodden upon. Pilot pricked up his ears when I came in: then he jumped up with

a yelp and a whine, and bounded towards me: he almost knocked the tray from my hands. I set it on the table; then patted him, and said softly, "Lie down!" Mr. Rochester turned mechanically to see what the commotion was: but as he saw nothing, he returned and sighed.

"Give me the water, Mary," he said.

I approached him with the now only half-filled glass. Pilot followed me, still excited.

"What is the matter?" he inquired.

"Down, Pilot!" I again said. He checked the water on its way to his lips, and seemed to listen: he drank, and put the glass down. "This is you, Mary, is it not?"

"Mary is in the kitchen," I answered.

He put out his hand with a quick gesture, but not seeing

where I stood, he did not touch me. "Who is this? Who is this?" he demanded, trying, as it seemed, to *see* with those sightless eyes—unavailing and distressing attempt! "Answer me—speak again!" he ordered, imperiously and aloud.

"Will you have a little more water, sir? I spilt half of what was in the glass," I said.

"*Who* is it? *What* is it? Who speaks?"

"Pilot knows me, and John and Mary know I am here. I came only this evening," I answered.

"Great God!—what delusion has come over me? What sweet madness has seized me?"

"No delusion—no madness: your mind, sir, is too strong for delusion, your health too sound for frenzy."

"And where is the speaker? Is it only a voice? Oh! I *cannot* see, but I must feel, or my heart will stop and my brain burst. Whatever—whoever you are—be

perceptible to the touch or I cannot live!"

He groped; I arrested his wandering hand, and prisoned it in both mine.

"Her very fingers!" he cried; "her small, slight fingers! If so, there must be more of her!"

The muscular hand broke from my custody; my arm was seized, my shoulder—neck—waist—I was entwined and gathered to him.

"Is it Jane? *What* is it? This is her shape—this is her size—"

"And this her voice," I added. "She is all here: her heart, too. God bless you, sir! I am glad to be so near you again."

"Jane Eyre—Jane Eyre," was all he said.

"My dear master," I answered, "I am Jane Eyre: I have found you out—I am come back to you."

"In truth—in the flesh? My living Jane?"

"You touch me, sir,—you hold me, and fast enough: I am not like a corpse, nor vacant like air, am I?"

"My living darling! These are certainly her limbs, and these her features; but I cannot be so blest, after all my misery. It is a dream; such dreams as I have had at night when I have clasped her once more to my heart, as I do now; and kissed her, as thus—and felt that she loved me, and trusted that she would not leave me."

"Which I never will, sir, from this day."

"Never will, says the vision? But I always woke and found it an empty mockery; and I was desolate and abandoned—my life dark, lonely, hopeless—my soul athirst and forbidden to drink—my heart famished and never to be fed. Gentle, soft dream, nestling in my arms now, you will fly, too, as your sisters have all fled before you: but kiss me before you go—embrace me, Jane."

"There, sir—and there!"

I pressed my lips to his once brilliant and now rayless eyes—I swept his hair from his brow, and kissed that too. he suddenly seemed to arouse himself: the conviction of the reality of all this seized him.

"It is you—is it, Jane? You are come back to me, then?"

"I am."

"And you do not lie dead in some ditch under some stream? And you are not a pining outcast amongst strangers?"

"No, sir; I am an independent woman now."

"Independent! What do you mean, Jane?"

"My uncle in Madeira is dead, and he left me five thousand pounds."

"Ah, this is practical—this is real!" he cried: "I should never dream that. Besides, there is that peculiar voice of hers, so animating and piquant, as well as soft: it cheers my withered heart; it puts life into it.—What, Janet! Are you an independent woman? A rich woman?"

"Quite rich, sir. If you won't let me live with you, I can build a house of my own close up to your door, and you may come and sit in my parlour when you want company of an evening."

"But as you are rich, Jane, you have now, no doubt, friends who will look after you, and not suffer you to devote yourself to a blind lamenter like me?"

"I told you I am independent, sir, as well as rich: I am my own mistress."

"And you will stay with me?"

"Certainly—unless you object. I will be your neighbour, your nurse, your house-keeper. I find you lonely: I will be your companion—to read to you, to walk with you, to sit with you, to wait on you, to

be eyes and hands to you. Cease to look so melancholy, my dear master; you shall not be left desolate, so long as I live."

He replied not: he seemed serious— abstracted; he sighed; he half-opened his lips as if to speak: he closed them again. I felt a little embarrassed. Perhaps I had too rashly overleaped conventionalities; and he, like St. John, saw impropriety in my inconsiderateness. I had indeed made my proposal from the idea that he wished and would ask me to be his wife: an expectation, not the less certain because unexpressed, had buoyed me up, that he would claim me at once as his own. But no hint to that effect escaping him and his countenance becoming more overcast, I suddenly remembered that I might have been all wrong, and was perhaps playing the fool unwittingly; and I began gently to withdraw myself from his arms—but he eagerly snatched me closer.

"No—no—Jane; you must not go. No—

I have touched you, heard you, felt the comfort of your presence—the sweetness of your consolation: I cannot give up these joys. I have little left in myself—I must have you. The world may laugh—may call me absurd, selfish—but it does not signify. My very soul demands you: it will be satisfied: or it will take deadly vengeance on its frame."

"Well, sir, I will stay with you: I have said so."

"Yes—but you understand one thing by staying with me: and I understand another. You, perhaps, could make up your mind to be about my hand and chair—to wait on me as a kind little nurse (for you have an affectionate heart and a generous spirit, which prompt you to make sacrifices for those you pity), and that ought to suffice for me, no doubt. I suppose I should now entertain none but fatherly feelings for you: do you think so? Come—tell me."

"I will think what you like, sir: I am content to be only your nurse, if you think it better."

"But you cannot always be my nurse, Janet: you are young—you must marry one day."

"I don't care about being married."

"You should care, Janet: if I were what I once was, I would try to make you care—but—a sightless block!"

He relapsed again into gloom. I, on the contrary, became more cheerful, and took fresh courage: these last words gave me an insight as to where the difficulty lay; and as it was no difficulty with me, I felt quite relieved from my previous embarrassment. I resumed a livelier vein of conversation.

"It is time some one undertook to rehumanise you," said I, parting his thick and long uncut locks; "for I see you are being metamorphosed into a lion, or something of that sort. You have a 'faux air' of Nebuchadnezzar in the fields about you, that is certain: your hair reminds me of eagles' feathers; whether your nails are grown like birds' claws or not, I have not yet noticed."

"On this arm, I have neither hand nor nails," he said, drawing the mutilated limb from his breast, and showing it to me. "It is a mere stump—a ghastly sight! Don't you think so, Jane?"

"It is a pity to see it; and a pity to see your eyes—and the scar of fire on your forehead: and the worst of it is, one is in danger of loving you too well for all this; and making too much of you."

"I thought you would be revolted, Jane, when you saw my arm, and my cicatrised visage."

"Did you? Don't tell me so—lest I should say something disparaging to your judgment. Now, let me leave you an instant, to make a better fire, and have the hearth swept up. Can you tell when there is a good fire?"

"Yes; with the right eye I see a glow—a ruddy haze."

"And you see the candles?"

"Very dimly—each is a luminous cloud."

"Can you see me?"

"No, my fairy: but I am only too thankful to hear and feel you."

"When do you take supper?"

"I never take supper."

"But you shall have some to-night. I am hungry: so are you, I daresay, only you forget."

Summoning Mary, I soon had the room in more cheerful order: I prepared him, likewise, a comfortable repast. My spirits were excited, and with pleasure and ease I talked to him during supper, and for a long time after. There was no harassing restraint, no repressing of glee and vivacity with him; for with him I was at perfect ease, because I knew I suited him: all I said or did seemed either to console or revive him. Delightful consciousness! It brought to life and light my whole nature: in his presence I thoroughly lived; and he lived in mine. Blind as he was, smiles played over his face, joy dawned on his forehead: his lineaments softened and warmed.

After supper, he began to ask me many questions, of where I had been, what I had been doing, how I had found him out; but I gave him only very partial replies: it was too late to enter into particulars that night. Besides, I wished to touch no deep-thrilling chord—to open no fresh well of emotion in his heart: my sole present aim was to cheer him. Cheered, as I have said, he was: and yet but by fits. If a moment's silence broke the conversation, he would turn restless, touch me, then say, "Jane."

"You are altogether a human being, Jane? You are certain of that?"

"I conscientiously believe so, Mr. Rochester."

"Yet how, on this dark and doleful evening, could you so suddenly rise on my lone hearth? I stretched my hand to take a glass of water from a hireling, and it was given me by you: I asked a question, expecting John's wife to answer me, and your voice spoke at my ear."

"Because I had come in, in Mary's stead, with the tray."

"And there is enchantment in the very hour I am now spending with you. Who can tell what a dark, dreary, hopeless life I have dragged on for months past? Doing nothing, expecting nothing; merging night in day; feeling but the sensation of cold when I let the fire go out, of hunger when I forgot to eat: and then a ceaseless sorrow, and, at times, a very delirium of desire to behold my Jane again. Yes: for her restoration I longed, far more than for that of my lost sight. How can it be that Jane is with me, and says she loves me? Will she not depart as suddenly as she came? To-morrow, I fear I shall find her no more."

A common-place, practical reply, out of the train of his own disturbed ideas, was, I was sure, the best and most reassuring for him in this frame of mind. I passed my finger over his eyebrows, and remarked that they were scorched, and that I would apply something which should make them grow as broad and black as ever.

"Where is the use of doing me good in any way, beneficent spirit, when, at some fatal moment, you will again desert me—passing like a shadow, whither and how to me unknown; and for me, remaining afterwards undiscoverable?"

"Have you a pocket-comb about you, sir?"

"What for, Jane?"

"Just to comb out this shaggy black mane. I find you rather alarming, when I examine you close at hand: you talk of my being a fairy; but I am sure, you are more like a brownie."

"Am I hideous, Jane?"

"Very, sir: you always were, you know."

"Humph! The wickedness has not been taken out of you, wherever you have sojourned."

"Yet I have been with good people; far better than you: a hundred times better people; possessed of ideas and views you never entertained in your life: quite more refined and exalted."

"Who the deuce have you been with?"

"If you twist in that way you will make me pull the hair out of your head; and then I think you will cease to entertain doubts of my substantiality."

144

"Who have you been with, Jane?"

"You shall not get it out of me to-night, sir; you must wait till to-morrow; to leave my tale half-told, will, you know, be a sort of security that I shall appear at your breakfast-table to finish it. By-the-by, I must mind not to rise on your hearth with only a glass of water, then: I must bring an egg at the least, to say nothing of fried ham."

"You mocking changeling—fairy-born and human-bred! You make me feel as I have not felt these twelve months. If Saul could have had you for his David, the evil spirit would have been exorcised without the aid of the harp."

"There, sir, you are redd up and made decent. Now I'll leave you: I have been travelling these last three days, and I believe I am tired. Good-night."

"Just one word, Jane: were there only ladies in the house where you have been?"

I laughed and made my escape, still laughing as I ran upstairs. "A good idea!" I thought, with glee. "I see I have the means of fretting him out of his melancholy for some time to come."

Very early the next morning, I heard him up and astir, wandering from one room to another. As soon as Mary came down I heard the question: "Is Miss Eyre here?" Then: "Which room did you put her into? Was it dry? Is she up? Go and ask if she wants anything: and when she will come down."

I came down as soon as I thought there was a prospect of breakfast. Entering the room very softly, I had a view of him before he discovered my presence. It was mournful, indeed, to witness the subjugation of that vigorous spirit to a corporeal infirmity. He sat in his chair,—still, but not at rest: expectant evidently; the lines of now habitual sadness marking his strong features. His countenance reminded one of a lamp

145

quenched, waiting to be relit—and alas! it was not himself that could now kindle the lustre of animated expression: he was dependent on another for that office! I had meant to be gay and careless, but the powerlessness of the strong man touched my heart to the quick: still I accosted him with what vivacity I could:—

"It is a bright, sunny morning, sir," I said. "The rain is over and gone, and there is a tender shining after it: you shall have a walk soon."

I had wakened the glow: his features beamed.

"Oh, you are indeed there, my skylark! Come to me. You are not gone: not vanished? I heard one of your kind an hour ago, singing high over the wood: but its song had no music for me, any more than the rising sun had rays. All the melody on earth is concentrated in my Jane's tongue to my ear (I am glad it is not naturally a silent one): all the sunshine I can feel is in her presence."

The water stood in my eyes to hear this avowal of his dependence: just as if a royal eagle, chained to a perch, should be forced to entreat a sparrow to become its purveyor. But I would not be lachrymose: I dashed off the salt drops, and busied myself with preparing breakfast.

Most of the morning was spent in the open air. I led him out of the wet and wild wood into some cheerful fields: I described to him how brilliantly green they were; how the flowers and hedges looked refreshed; how sparklingly blue was the sky. I sought a seat for him in a hidden and lovely spot: a dry stump of a tree; nor did I refuse to let him, when seated, place me on his knee: why should I, when both he and I were happier near than apart? Pilot lay beside us: all was quiet. He broke out suddenly while clasping me in his arms:—

"Cruel, cruel deserter! Oh, Jane, what

146

did I feel when I discovered you had fled from Thornfield, and when I could nowhere find you; and, after examining your apartment, ascertained that you had taken no money, nor anything which could serve as an equivalent! A pearl necklace I had given you lay untouched in its little casket; your trunks were left corded and locked as they had been prepared for the bridal tour. What could my darling do, I asked, left destitute and penniless? And what did she do? Let me hear now."

Thus urged, I began the narrative of my experience for the last year. I softened considerably what related to the three days of wandering and starvation, because to have told him all would have been to inflict unnecessary pain: the little I did say lacerated his faithful heart deeper than I wished.

I should not have left him thus, he said, without any means of making my way: I should have told him my intention. I should have confided in him: he would never have forced me to be his mistress. Violent as he had seemed in his despair, he, in truth, loved me far too well and too tenderly to constitute himself my tyrant: he would have given me half his fortune, without demanding so much as a kiss in return, rather than I should have flung myself friendless on the wide world. I had endured, he was certain, more than I had confessed to him.

"Well, whatever my sufferings had been, they were very short," I answered: and then I proceeded to tell him how I had been received at Moor House; how I had obtained the office of schoolmistress, etc. The accession of fortune, the discovery of my relations, followed in due order. Of course, St. John Rivers' name came in frequently in the progress of my tale. When I had done, that name was immediately taken up.

"This St. John, then, is your cousin?"

"Yes."

You have spoken of him often: did you like him?"

"He was a very good man, sir; I could not help liking him."

"A good man? Does that mean a respectable, well-conducted man of fifty? Or what does it mean?"

"St. John was only twenty-nine, sir,"

"'*Jeune encore,*' as the French say. Is he a person of low stature, phlegmatic, and plain? A person whose goodness consists rather in his guiltlessness of vice, than in his prowess in virtue?"

"He is untiringly active. Great and exalted deeds are what he lives to perform."

"But his brain? That is probably rather soft? He meant well: but you shrug your shoulders to hear him talk?"

"He talks little, sir: what he does say is ever to the point. His brain is first-rate, I should think not impressible, but vigorous."

"Is he an able man, then?"

"Truly able."

"A thoroughly educated man?"

"St. John is an accomplished an profound scholar."

"His manners, I think, you said are not to your taste?—priggish and parsonic?"

"I never mentioned his manners; but, unless I had a very bad taste, they must suit it; they are polished, calm, and gentlemanlike."

"His appearance,—I forget what description you gave of his appearance;—a sort of raw curate, half strangled with his white neckcloth, and stilted up on his thick-soled high-lows, eh?"

"St. John dresses well. he is a handsome man: tall, fair with blue eyes, and a Grecian profile."

149

(Aside.) "Damn him!"—(To me.) "Did you like him, Jane?

"Yes, Mr. Rochester, I liked him: but you asked me that before."

I perceived, of course, the drift of my interlocutor. Jealousy had got hold of him: she stung him; but the sting was salutary: it gave him respite from the gnawing fang of melancholy. I would not, therefore, immediately charm the snake.

"Perhaps you would rather not sit any longer on my knee, Miss Eyre?" was the next somewhat unexpected observation.

"Why not, Mr. Rochester?"

"The picture you have just drawn is suggestive of a rather too overwhelming contrast. Your words have delineated very prettily a graceful Apollo: he is present to your imagination,—tall, fair, blue-eyed, and with a Grecian profile. Your eyes dwell on a Vulcan,—a real blacksmith, brown, broad-shouldered; and blind and lame into the bargain."

"I never thought of it, before; but you certainly are rather like Vulcan, sir."

"Well,—you can leave me, ma'am: but before you go" (and he retained me by a firmer grasp than ever, "you will be pleased just to answer me a question or two." He paused.

"What questions, Mr. Rochester?"

Then followed this cross-examination.

"St. John made you schoolmistress of Morton before he knew you were his cousin?"

"Yes."

"You would often see him? He would visit the school sometimes?"

"Daily."

"He would approve of your plans, Jane? I know they would be clever, for you are a talented creature."

"He approved of them—yes."

"He would discover many things in you he could not have expected to find? Some of your accomplishments are not ordinary."

"I don't know about that."

"You had a little cottage near the school, you say: did he ever come there to see you?"

"Now and then."

"Of an evening?"

"Once or twice."

A pause.

"How long did you reside with him and his sisters after the cousinship was discovered?"

"Five months."

"Did Rivers spend much time with the ladies of his family?"

"Yes; the back parlour was both his study and ours: he sat near the window, and we by the table."

"Did he study much?"

"A good deal."

"What?"

"Hindostanee."

"And what did you do meantime?"

"I learnt German, at first."

"Did he teach you?"

"He did not understand German."

"Did he teach you nothing?"

"A little Hindostanee."

"Rivers taught you Hindostanee?"

"Yes, sir."

"And his sisters also?"

"No."

"Only you?"

"Only me."

"Did you ask to learn?"

"No."

"He wished to teach you?"

"Yes."

A second pause.

"Why did he wish it? Of what use could Hindostanee be to you?"

"He intended me to go with him to India."

"Ah! here I reach the root of the matter. He wanted you to marry him?"

"He asked me to marry him."

"That is a fiction—an impudent invention to vex me."

"I beg your pardon, it is the literal truth: he asked me more than once, and was as stiff about urging his point as ever you could be."

"Miss Eyre, I repeat it, you can leave me. How often am I to say the same thing? Why do you remain pertinaciously perched on my knee, when I have given you notice to quit?"

"Because I am comfortable there."

"No, Jane, you are not comfortable there, because your heart is not with me: it is with this cousin—this St. John. Oh, till this moment, I thought my little Jane was all mine! I had a belief she loved me even when she left me: that was an atom of sweet in much bitter. Long as we have been parted, hot tears as I have wept over our separation, I never thought that while I was mourning her, she was loving another! But it is useless grieving. Jane, leave me: go and marry Rivers."

"Shake me off, then, sir,—push me away, for I'll not leave you of my own accord."

"Jane, I ever like your tone of voice: it still renews hope, it sounds so truthful. When I hear it, it carries me back a year. I forget that you have formed a new tie. But I am not a fool—go——"

"Where must I go, sir?"

"Your own way—with the husband you have chosen."

"Who is that?"

"You know—this St. John Rivers."

"He is not my husband, nor ever will be. He does not love me: I do not love him. He loves (as he *can* love, and that is not as you love) a beautiful young lady called Rosamond. He wanted to marry me only because he thought I should

152

make a suitable missionary's wife, which she would not have done. He is good and great, but severe; and, for me, cold as an iceberg. He is not like you, sir: I am not happy at his side, nor near him, nor with him. He has no indulgence for me—no fondness. He sees nothing attractive in me; not even youth—only a few useful mental points.—Then I must leave you, sir, to go to him?"

I shuddered involuntarily, and clung instinctively closer to my blind but beloved master. He smiled.

"What, Jane! Is this true? Is such really the state of matters between you and Rivers?"

"Absolutely, sir. Oh, you need not be jealous! I wanted to tease you a little to make you less sad: I thought anger would be better than grief. But if you wish me to love you, could you but see how much I *do* love you, you would be proud and content. All my heart is yours, sir: it belongs to you; and with you it would remain, were fate to exile the rest of me from your presence for ever."

Again, as he kissed me, painful thoughts darkened his aspect.

"My seared vision! My crippled strength!" he murmured regretfully.

I caressed, in order to soothe him. I knew of what he was thinking, and wanted to speak for him; but dared not. As he turned aside his face a minute, I saw a tear slide from under the sealed eyelid, and trickle down the manly cheek. My

153

heart swelled.

"I am no better than the old lightning-struck chestnut-tree in Thornfield orchard," he remarked, erelong. "And what right would that ruin have to bid a budding woodbine cover its decay with freshness?"

"You are no ruin, sir—no lightning-struck tree: you are green and vigorous. Plants will grow about your roots, whether you ask them or not, because they take delight in your bountiful shadow; and as they grow they will lean towards you, and wind round you, because your strength offers them so safe a prop."

Again he smiled: I gave him comfort.

"You speak of friends, Jane?" he asked.

"Yes; of friends," I answered, rather hesitatingly: for I knew I meant more than friends, but could not tell what other word to employ. He helped me!

"Ah! Jane. But I want a wife."

"Do you, sir?"

"Yes: is it news to you?"

"Of course: you said nothing about it before."

"Is it unwelcome news?"

"That depends on circumstances, sir—on your choice."

"Which you shall make for me, Jane. I will abide by your decision."

"Choose then, sir—*her who loves you best.*"

"I will at least choose—*her I love best.* Jane, will you marry me?"

"Yes, sir."

"A poor blind man, whom you will have to lead about by the hand?"

"Yes, sir."

"A crippled man, twenty years older than you, whom you will have to wait on?"

"Yes, sir."

"Truly, Jane?"

"Most truly, sir."

"Oh! my darling! God bless and reward you!"

155

"Mr. Rochester, if ever I did a good deed in my life—if ever I thought a good thought—if ever I prayed a sincere and blameless prayer—if ever I wished a righteous wish,—I am rewarded now. To be your wife is, for me, to be as happy as I can be on earth."

"Because you delight in sacrifice."

"Sacrifice! What do I sacrifice? Famine for food, expectation for content. To be privileged to put my arms round what I value—to press my lips to what I love— to repose on what I trust: is that to make a sacrifice? If so, then certainly I delight in sacrifice."

"And to bear with my infirmities, Jane: to overlook my deficiencies."

"Which are none, sir, to me. I love you better now, when I can really be useful to you, than I did in your state of proud independence, when you disdained every part but that of the giver and protector."

"Hitherto I have hated to be helped— to be led: henceforth, I feel, I shall hate it no more. I did not like to put my hand into a hireling's, but it is pleasant to feel it circled by Jane's little fingers. I preferred utter loneliness to the constant attendance of servants; but Jane's soft ministry will be a perpetual joy. Jane suits me: do I suit her?"

"To the finest fibre of my nature, sir."

"The case being so, we have nothing in the world to wait for: we must be married instantly."

He looked and spoke with eagerness: his old impetuosity was rising.

"We must become one flesh without any delay, Jane: there is but the license to get—then we marry."

"Mr. Rochester, I have just discovered the sun is far declined from its meridian, and Pilot is actually gone home to his dinner. Let me look at your watch."

"Fasten it into your girdle, Janet, and keep it henceforward: I have no use for it."

"It is nearly four o'clock in the afternoon, sir. Don't you feel hungry?"

"The third day from this must be our wedding-day, Jane. Never mind fine clothes and jewels, now: all that is not worth a fillip."

"The sun has dried up all the raindrops, sir. The breeze is still: it is quite hot."

"Do you know, Jane, I have your little pearl necklace at this moment fastened round my bronze scrag under my cravat? I have worn it since the day I lost my

only treasure: as a memento of her."

"We will go home through the wood: that will be the shadiest way."

He put me off his knee, rose, and reverently lifting his hat from his brow and bending his sightless eyes to the earth, he stood in mute devotion. Only the last words of the worship were audible.

"I thank my Maker, that in the midst of judgment he has remembered mercy. I humbly entreat my Redeemer to give me strength to lead henceforth a purer life than I have done hitherto!"

Then he stretched his hand out to be led. I took that dear hand, held it a moment to my lips, then let it pass round my shoulder: being so much lower of stature than he, I served both for his prop and guide. We entered the wood, and wended homeward.

When You Are Old
William Butler Yeats

When you are old and grey and full of sleep,
And nodding by the fire, take down this book,
And slowly read, and dream of the soft look
Your eyes had once, and of their shadows deep;

How many loved your moments of glad grace,
And loved your beauty with love false or true,
But one man loved the pilgrim soul in you,
And loved the sorrows of your changing face;

And bending down beside the glowing bars,
Murmur, a little sadly, how Love fled
And paced upon the mountains overhead
And hid his face amid a crowd of stars.

Letters between Robert and Elizabeth Barrett Browning

TO ELIZABETH   *January 10, 1845*

I love your verses with all my heart, dear Miss Barrett,—and this is no off-hand complimentary letter that I shall write,—whatever else, no prompt matter-of-course recognition of your genius and there a graceful and natural end of the thing: since the day last week when I first read your poems, I quite laugh to remember how I have been turning and turning again in my mind what I should be able to tell you of their effect upon me—for in the first flush of delight I thought I would this once get out of my habit of purely passive enjoyment, when I do really enjoy, and thoroughly justify my admiration—perhaps even, as a loyal fellow-craftsman should, try and find fault and do you some little good to be proud of hereafter! —but nothing comes of it all—so into me has it gone, and part of me has it become, this great living poetry of yours, not a flower of which but took root and grew. . . oh, how different that is from lying to be dried and pressed flat and prized highly and

Robert and Elizabeth Barrett Browning

put in a book with a proper account at top and bottom, and shut up and put away. . . and the book called a "Flora," besides! After all, I need not give up the thought of doing that, too, in time; because even now, talking with whoever is worthy, I can give a reason for my faith in one and another excellence, the fresh strange music, the affluent language, the exquisite pathos and true new brave thought— but in this addressing myself to you, your own self, and for the first time, my felling rises altogether. I do, as I say, love these Books with all my heart—and I love you too: do you know I was once not very far from seeing—really seeing you? Mr. Kenyorh said to me one morning "would you like to see Miss Barrett?"—then he went to announce me,—then he returned. . . you were too unwell—and now it is years ago—and I feel as at some untoward passage in my travels—as if I had been close, so close, to some world's-wonder in chapel or crypt,. . . only a screen to push and I might have entered— but there was some slight. . . so it now seems. . . slight and just-sufficient bar to admission, and the half-opened door shut, and I went home my thousands of miles, and the sight was never

163

Robert and Elizabeth Barrett Browning

to be! Well, these Poems were to be—and this true thankful joy
and pride with which I feel myself.

TO ROBERT   *January 10, 1846*

It seems to me, to myself, that no man was ever before to any
woman what you are to me—the fulness must be in proportion, you
know, to the vacancy. . . and only I know what was behind—the long
wilderness without the blossoming rose. . . and the capacity for
happiness, like a black gaping hole, before this silver flooding. Is it
wonderful that I should stand as in a dream, and disbelieve—not
you—but my own fate? Was ever any one taken suddenly from a
lampless dungeon and placed upon the pinnacle of a mountain, without the head turning round and the heart turning faint, as mine do?

*A spinal injury left Elizabeth Barrett Browning in a
wheelchair at age 15. However, the publication of her
poetry in 1844 attracted the attentions of fellow poet,
Robert Browning. The couple eloped to Italy in 1846
and lived happily there until her death in 1861.*

Looking for Your Face
Rumi

From the beginning of my life
I have been looking for your face
but today I have seen it

Today I have seen
the charm, the beauty,
the unfathomable grace
of the face
that I was looking for

Today I have found you
and those who laughed
and scorned me yesterday
are sorry that they were not looking
as I did

I am bewildered by the magnificence
of your beauty
and wish to see you
with a hundred eyes

My heart has burned with passion
and has searched forever
for this wondrous beauty
that I now behold

I am ashamed to
call this love human
and afraid of God
to call it divine

Your fragrant breath
like the morning breeze
has come to the stillness of the garden
You have breathed new life into me
I have become your sunshine
and also your shadow

My soul is screaming in ecstasy
Every fiber of my being
is in love with you

Your effulgence
has lit a fire in my heart
and you have made radiant for me
the earth and sky

My arrow of love
has arrived at the target
I am in the house of mercy
and my heart
is a place of prayer

Heavenly Truffles

*C*hocolate is, of course, the food of love. Take your pick between Hazelnut and Milk Chocolate or make them both and mix them up. Either way, a batch of truffles is the perfect gift to say "I Love You" any day of the year.

Hazelnut Truffles

1/4 cup heavy whipping cream
4 oz. bittersweet chocolate and semi-sweet chocolate, finely chopped
2 tablespoons unsalted butter
2 tablespoons Nutella or other hazelnut spread
3/4 cup hazelnuts, chopped

1. Bring 1/2 inch of water to a simmer in a skillet.
2. In a saucepan that is slightly smaller than the skillet, bring cream to a simmer over medium heat and add chocolate, butter, and Nutella.
3. Place chocolate mixture over simmering water and stir constantly until chocolate is completely melted.
4. Remove from heat and transfer to a shallow bowl.
5. Cover and refrigerate until set, about two hours.
6. Remove chocolate from refrigerator.
7. Line a baking sheet with parchment (or wax) paper.
8. Using a melon-baller or small spoon, scrape along the surface of the chocolate and use your hands to shape 1-inch balls.
9. Roll balls in chopped hazelnuts. (Note: If chopped hazelnuts are unavailable, prepare them yourself by placing whole, unroasted nuts on a cookie sheet in a preheated 275°F oven for 20–30 minutes. When skins begin to crack, remove nuts from oven, pour them into a clean kitchen towel, and allow them to steam for 3–5 minutes. Then vigorously rub nuts in towel until skin flakes off, about two minutes. Chop in food processor to a fine dice. Be careful not to over-chop or you'll end up with hazelnut butter!)

10. Truffles can be stored between layers of parchment or wax paper, covered tightly, and refrigerated for up to two weeks (or frozen up to 3 months).

Makes about 30 truffles

Milk Chocolate Truffles

6 oz. milk chocolate, chopped
2 oz. semi-sweet chocolate, chopped
2 tablespoons unsalted butter
1/3 cup unsweetened cocoa

1. In a double boiler, melt chocolate and butter together, stirring constantly.
2. Once melted, transfer mixture to a shallow bowl and refrigerate until set, about 2 hours.
3. Pour cocoa into a pie plate or small bowl.
4. Line a baking sheet with parchment or wax paper.
5. Using a melon-baller or small spoon, scrape along the surface of chocolate and use your hands to shape 1-inch balls.
6. Roll balls in cocoa, and place on baking sheet.
7. Truffles can be stored between layers of parchment or wax paper, covered tightly, and refrigerated for up to two weeks (or frozen up to 3 months).

Makes about 30 truffles

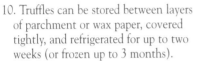

169

To My Dear and Loving Husband
Anne Bradstreet

If ever two were one, then surely we.
If ever man were loved by wife, then thee;
If ever wife was happy in a man,
Compare with me ye women if you can.
I prize thy love more than whole mines of gold,
Or all the riches that the East doth hold.
My love is such that rivers cannot quench,
Nor ought but love from thee, give recompense.
Thy love is such I can no way repay,
The heavens reward thee manifold I pray.
Then while we live, in love let's so persevere,
That when we live no more, we may live ever.

from the writings of...
Carl Jung

The young person of marriageable age does, of course, possess an ego-consciousness (girls more than men, as a rule), but, since he has only recently emerged from the mists of original unconsciousness, he is certain to have wide areas which still lie in the shadow and which preclude to that extent the formation of psychological relationship. This means, in practice, that the young man (or woman) can have only an incomplete understanding of himself and others, and is therefore imperfectly informed as to his, and their, motives. As a rule the motives he acts from are largely uncon-

from the writings of… Carl Jung

scious. Subjectively, of course, he thinks himself very conscious and knowing, for we constantly overestimate the existing content of consciousness, and it is a great and surprising discovery when we find that what we had supposed to be the final peak is nothing but the first step in a very long climb. The greater the area of unconsciousness, the less is marriage a matter of free choice, as is shown subjectively in the fatal com-pulsion one feels so acutely when one is in love.

from "Marriage as a Psychological Relationship," 1925

Psychiatrist Carl Gustav Jung met Emma Rauschenbach in 1893 and prophesied that they would marry. Ten years later, in 1903, they were, and stayed happily married for 52 years.

Summer

Edith Wharton

Charity's heart contracted. The first fall of night after a day of radiance often gave her a sense of hidden menace: it was like looking out over the world as it would be when love had gone from it. She wondered if some day she would sit in that same place and watch in vain for her lover....

His bicycle-bell sounded down the lane, and in a minute she was at the gate and his eyes were laughing at hers. They walked back through the long grass, and pushed open the door behind the house. The room at first seemed quite dark and they had to grope their way in hand-in-hand. Through the window-frame the sky looked light by contrast, and above the black mass of asters in the earthen jar one white star glimmered like a moth.

'There was such a lot to do at the last minute,' Harney was explaining, 'and I had to drive down to Creston to meet someone who has come to stay with my cousin for the show.'

He had his arms about her, and his kisses were in her hair and her lips. Under his touch things deep down in her struggled to the light and sprang up like flowers in sunshine. She twisted her fingers into his, and they sat down side by side on the improvised couch. She hardly heard his excuses for being late: in his absence a thousand doubts tormented her, but as soon as he appeared she ceased to wonder where he had come from, what had delayed him, who had kept him from her. It seemed as if the places he had been in, and the people he had been with, must cease to exist when he left them, just as her own life was suspended in his absence.

He continued, now, to talk to her volubly and gaily, deploring his lateness, grumbling at the demands on his time, and good-humoredly mimicking Miss Hatchard's benevolent agitation. 'She hurried off Miles to ask Mr. Royall to speak at the Town Hall tomorrow: I didn't know till it was done.' Charity was silent, and he added: 'After all, perhaps it's just as well. No one else could have done it.'

Charity made no answer: She did not care what part her guardian played in the morrow's ceremonies. Like all the other figures peopling her meager world he had grown non-existent to her. She had even put off hating him.

'Tomorrow I shall only see you from far off,' Harney continued. 'But in the evening there'll be the dance in the Town Hall. Do you want me to promise not to dance with any other girl?'

Any other girl? Were there any others? She had forgotten even that peril, so enclosed did he and she seem in their secret world. Her heart gave a frightened jerk.

'Yes, promise.'

He laughed and took her in his arms. 'You goose—not even if they're hideous?'

He pushed the hair from her forehead, bending her face back, as his way was, and leaning over so that his head loomed black between her eyes and the paleness of the sky, in which the white star floated...

I Want You
Arthur L. Gillom

I want you when the shades of eve are falling
 And purple shadows drift across the land;
When sleepy birds to loving mates are calling—
 I want the soothing softness of your hand.

I want you when the stars shine up above me,
 And Heaven's flooded with the bright moonlight;
I want you with your arms and lips to love me
 Throughout the wonder watches of the night.

I want you when in dreams I still remember
 The ling'ring of your kiss—for old times' sake—
With all your gentle ways, so sweetly tender,
 I want you in the morning when I wake.

I want you when the day is at its noontime,
  Sun-steeped and quiet, or drenched with sheets of rain;
I want you when the roses bloom in June-time;
  I want you when the violets come again.

I want you when my soul is thrilled with passion;
  I want you when I'm weary and depressed;
I want you when in lazy, slumbrous fashion
  My senses need the haven of your breast.

I want you when through field and wood I'm roaming;
  I want you when I'm standing on the shore;
I want you when the summer birds are homing—
  And when they've flown—I want you more and more.

I want you, dear, through every changing season;
  I want you with a tear or with a smile;
I want you more than any rhyme or reason—
  I want you, want you, want you—all the while.

I Only Have Eyes for You

Al Dubin and Harry Warren

My love must be a kind of blind love,
I can't see anyone but you.
And dear, I wonder if you find love
An optical illusion too?

Are the stars out to night?
I don't know if it's cloudy or bright
'Cause I only have eyes for you, dear.
The moon may be high, but I can't see a thing in the sky,
'Cause I only have eyes for you.

I don't know if we're in a garden,
Or on a crowded avenue.
You are here, so am I,
Maybe millions of people go by,
But they all disappear from view,
And I only have eyes for you.

The Song of Solomon

(from the Old Testament)

I am the rose of Sharon, and the lily of the valleys.

As the lily among thorns, so is my love among the daughters.

As the apple tree among the trees of the wood, so is my beloved among the sons. I sat down under his shadow with great delight, and his fruit was sweet to my taste.

He brought me to the banqueting house, and his banner over me was love.

Stay me with flagons, comfort me with apples: for I am sick of love.

His left hand is under my head, and his right hand doth embrace me.

I charge you, O ye daughters of Jerusalem, by the roes, and by the hinds of the field, that ye stir not up, nor awake my love, till he please.

The voice of my beloved! behold, he cometh leaping upon the mountains, skipping upon the hills.

My beloved is like a roe or a young hart: behold, he standeth behind our wall, he looketh forth at the windows, showing himself through the lattice.

My beloved spake, and said unto me, Rise up, my love, my fair one, and come away.

For, lo, the winter is past, the rain is over and gone;

The flowers appear on the earth; the time of the singing of birds is come, and the voice of the turtle is heard in our land:

The fig tree putteth forth her green figs, and the vines with the tender grape give a good smell. Arise, my love, my fair one, and come away.

O my dove, that art in the clefts of the rock, in the secret places of the stairs, let me see thy countenance, let me hear thy voice; for sweet is thy voice, and thy countenance is comely.

Take us the foxes, the little foxes, that spoil the vines; for our vines have tender grapes.

My beloved is mine, and I am his: he feedeth among the lilies.

Until the day break, and the shadows flee away, turn, my beloved, and be thou like a roe or a young hart upon the mountains of Bether.

Letter from Isadora Duncan to Gordon Craig

Waves!

Darling—It is about 3 o'clock—I have been sitting up writing the Marvellous Book! Had a wonderful torrent of ideas falling overeach other—Don't know if they are of any worth.

Astounding what I feel when you are not here—become suddenly very severe—don't care for Eating or sleeping but filled with lovely feelings and twice as sensitive to sounds lights colors etc. It's all a matter of magnetic forces—Same things that keep the Earth Circling about the own in constant rhythmetical waves of attraction & repulsion making the Complete Harmony—Wonderful.

Aren't we wonderful—

Love Love Love Love Love

Waves—love waves—

I've been writing about dance waves sound waves light waves

188

Isadora Duncan to Gordon Craig

—all the same— How many thousand miles an hour do light & sound waves travel—So quick travel never-ceasing love waves from me to you— and from you to me— Distance doesn't matter because the supply is never ceasing—Only the near touch is something too and I want that. Living with you makes me feel so Strong I think I could easily own the Earth— Isn't it beautiful. The transfusion. I am filled with Force. It is You—

> Good Night Love—
> Your Isa Dora

American dancer Isadora Duncan first met English actor and stage designer, Gordon Craig, at a Berlin dance performance in 1904. In the succeeding 3 years, they shared abundant correspondence. After 1907, communication dwindled, and it stopped altogether with her death in 1919.

189

A Summer Love Poem
Nikki Giovanni

clouds float by on a summer sky
                      i hop scotch over to you
rainbows arch from ground to gold
                      i climb over to you
thunder grumbles   lightning tumbles and i bounce over to you
sun beams back and catches me
                    smiling over at you

Romeo and Juliet

William Shakespeare

ACT II, SCENE II

Romeo comes forward.

ROMEO.   He jests at scars that never felt a wound.
Enter Juliet above.

But soft, what light through yonder window breaks?
It is the east and Juliet is the sun!
Arise fair sun and kill the envious moon
Who is already sick and pale with grief
That thou her maid art far more fair than she.
Be not her maid since she is envious,
Her vestal livery is but sick and green
And none but fools do wear it. Cast it off.

It is my lady, O it is my love!
O that she knew she were!
She speaks, yet she says nothing. What of that?
Her eye discourses, I will answer it.
I am too bold. 'Tis not to me she speaks.
Two of the fairest stars in all the heaven,
Having some business, do entreat her eyes
To twinkle in their spheres till they return.
What if her eyes were there, they in her head?
The brightness of her cheek would shame those stars
As daylight doth a lamp. Her eyes in heaven
Would through the airy region stream so bright
That birds would sing and think it were not night.
See how she leans her cheek upon her hand.
O that I were a glove upon that hand
That I might touch that cheek.

JULIET.   Ay me.

ROMEO.   She speaks.

O speak again bright angel, for thou art
As glorious to this night, being o'er my head,
As is a winged messenger of heaven
Unto the white-upturned wondering eyes
Of mortals that fall back to gaze on him

When he bestrides the lazy-puffing clouds
And sails upon the bosom of the air.

JULIET. O Romeo, Romeo, wherefore art thou Romeo?
Deny thy father and refuse thy name.
Or if thou wilt not, be but sworn my love
And I'll no longer be a Capulet.

ROMEO. Shall I hear more, or shall I speak at this?

JULIET. 'Tis but thy name that is my enemy:
Thou art thyself, though not a Montague.
What's Montague? It is nor hand nor foot
Nor arm nor face nor any other part
Belonging to a man. O be some other name.
What's in a name? That which we call a rose
By any other word would smell as sweet;
So Romeo would, were he not Romeo call'd,
Retain that dear perfection which he owes
Without that title. Romeo, doff thy name,
And for thy name, which is no part of thee,
Take all myself.

ROMEO. I take thee at thy word.
Call me but love, and I'll be new baptis'd:
Henceforth I never will be Romeo.

JULIET. What man art thou that thus bescreen'd in night

196

So stumblest on my counsel?

ROMEO. By a name
I know not how to tell thee who I am:
My name, dear saint, is hateful to myself
Because it is an enemy to thee.
Had I it written, I would tear the word.

JULIET. My ears have yet not drunk a hundred words
Of thy tongue's uttering, yet I know the sound.
Art thou not Romeo, and a Montague?

ROMEO. Neither, fair maid, if either thee dislike.

JULIET. How cam'st thou hither, tell me, and wherfore?
The orchard walls are high and hard to climb,
And the place death, considering who thou art,
If any of my kinsmen find thee here.

ROMEO. With love's light wings did I o'erperch these walls,
For stony limits cannot hold love out,
And what love can do, that dares love attempt:
Therefore thy kinsmen are no stop to me.

JULIET. If they do see thee, they will murder thee.

ROMEO. Alack, there lies more peril in thine eye
Than twenty of their swords. Look thou but sweet
And I am proof against their enmity.

JULIET. I would not for the world they saw thee here.

ROMEO. I have night's cloak to hide me from their eyes,
    And but thou love me, let them find me here.
    My life were better ended by their hate
    Than death prorogued, wanting of thy love.

JULIET. By whose direction found'st thou out this place?

ROMEO. By love, that first did prompt me to enquire.
    He lent me counsel, and I lent him eyes.
    I am no pilot, yet wert thou as far
    As that vast shore wash'd with the farthest sea,
    I should adventure for such merchandise.

JULIET. Thou knowest the mask of night is on my face,
    Else would a maiden blush bepaint my cheek
    For that which thou hast heard me speak tonight.
    Fain would I dwell on form; fain, fain deny
    What I have spoke. But farewell, compliment.
    Dost thou love me? I know thou wilt say 'Ay',
    And I will take thy word. Yet, if thou swear'st,
    Thou mayst prove false. At lovers' perjuries,
    They say, Jove laughs. O gentle Romeo,
    If thou dost love, pronounce it faithfully.
    Or, if thou think'st I am too quickly won,
    I'll frown and be perverse and say thee nay,
    So thou wilt woo; but else, not for the world.

In truth, fair Montague, I am too fond,
And therefore thou mayst think my haviour light,
But trust me, gentleman, I'll prove more true
Than those that have more cunning to be strange.
I should have been more strange, I must confess,
But that thou overheard'st, ere I was ware,
My true-love passion; therefore pardon me,
And not impute this yielding to light love
Which the dark night hath so discovered.

ROMEO.   Lady, by yonder blessed moon I vow,
          That tips with silver all these fruit-tree tops—

JULIET.   O swear not by the moon, th'inconstant moon,
          That monthly changes in her circled orb,
          Lest that thy love prove likewise variable.

ROMEO.   What shall I swear by?

JULIET.   Do not swear at all.
          Or if thou wilt, swear by thy gracious self,
          Which is the god of my idolatry,
          And I'll believe thee.

ROMEO.   If my heart's dear love—

JULIET.   Well, do not swear. Although I joy in thee,
          I have no joy of this contract tonight:
          It is too rash, too unadvis'd, too sudden,

Too like the lightning, which doth cease to be
Ere one can say 'It lightens'. Sweet, good night.
This bud of love, by summer's ripening breath,
May prove a beauteous flower when next we meet.
Good night, good night. As sweet repose and rest
Come to thy heart as that within my breast.

ROMEO. O wilt thou leave me so unsatisfied?

JULIET. What satisfaction canst thou have tonight?

ROMEO. Th'exchange of thy love's faithful vow for mine.

JULIET. I gave thee mine before thou didst request it,
And yet I would it were to give again.

ROMEO. Wouldst thou withdraw it? For what purpose, love?

JULIET. But to be frank and give it thee again;
And yet I wish but for the thing I have.
My bounty is as boundless as the sea,
My love as deep: the more I give to thee
The more I have, for both are infinite.
I hear some noise within. Dear love, adieu.

Nurse calls within.

Anon, good Nurse—Sweet Montague be true.
Stay but a little, I will come again. (*Exit Juliet.*)

ROMEO. O blessed blessed night. I am afeard,
Being in night, all this is but a dream,

Too flattering sweet to be substantial.

Enter Juliet above.

JULIET.   Three words, dear Romeo, and good night indeed.
        If that thy bent of love be honourable,
        Thy purpose marriage, send me word tomorrow
        By one that I'll procure to come to thee,
        Where and what time thou wilt perform the rite,
        And all my fortunes at thy foot I'll lay,
        And follow thee my lord throughout the world.

NURSE.   *(Within.)* Madam.

JULIET.   I come, anon—But if thou meanest not well
        I do beseech thee—

NURSE.   *(Within.)* Madam.

JULIET.   By and by I come—
        To cease thy strife and leave me to my grief.
        Tomorrow will I send.

ROMEO.   So thrive my soul—

JULIET.   A thousand times good night. *(Exit Juliet.)*

ROMEO.   A thousand times the worse, to want thy light.
        Love goes toward love as schoolboys from their books,
        But love from love, toward school with heavy looks.

Enter Juliet (above) again.

JULIET.   Hist! Romeo, hist! O for a falconer's voice

To lure this tassel-gentle back again.
Bondage is hoarse and may not speak aloud,
Else would I tear the cave where Echo lies
And make her airy tongue more hoarse than mine
With repetition of my Romeo's name.

ROMEO. It is my soul that calls upon my name.
How silver-sweet sound lovers' tongues by night,
Like softest music to attending ears.

JULIET. Romeo.

ROMEO. My nyas.

JULIET. What o'clock tomorrow
Shall I send to thee?

ROMEO. By the hour of nine.

JULIET. I will not fail. 'Tis twenty year till then.
I have forgot why I did call thee back.

ROMEO. Let me stand here till thou remember it.

JULIET. I shall forget, to have thee still stand there,
Remembering how I love thy company.

ROMEO. And I'll still stay to have thee still forget,
Forgetting any other home but this.

JULIET. 'Tis almost morning, I would have thee gone,
And yet no farther than a wanton's bird,
That lets it hop a little from his hand

            Like a poor prisoner in his twisted gyves,
            And with a silken thread plucks it back again,
            So loving-jealous of his liberty.

ROMEO.   I would I were thy bird.

JULIET.   Sweet, so would I:
            Yet I should kill thee with much cherishing.
            Good night, good night. Parting is such sweet sorrow
            That I shall say good night till it be morrow.

Exit Juliet.

ROMEO.   Sleep dwell upon thine eyes, peace in thy breast.
            Would I were sleep and peace so sweet to rest.
            The grey-ey'd morn smiles on the frowning night
            Chequering the eastern clouds with streaks of light;
            And darkness fleckled like a drunkard reels
            From forth day's pathway, make by Titan's wheels.
            Hence will I to my ghostly Sire's close cell,
            His help to crave and my dear hap to tell.

Exit.

I Loved You First
Christina Rossetti

Poca favilla gran fiamma seconda. —Dante.
Ogni altra cosa, ogni pensier va fore,
E sol ivi con voi rimansi amore. —Petrarca.

I loved you first: but afterwards your love
    Outsoaring mine, sang such a loftier song
As drowned the friendly cooings of my dove.
    Which owes the other most? My love was long,
    And yours one moment seemed to wax more strong;
I loved and guessed at you, you construed me
And loved me for what might or might not be—
    Nay, weights and measures do us both a wrong.
For verily love knows not "mine" or "thine,";
    With separate "I" and "thou" free love has done,
    For one is both and both are one in love:
Rich love knows nought of "thine that is not mine";
    Both have the strength and both the length thereof,
    Both of us, of the love which makes us one.

Let's Do It (Let's Fall In Love)

Cole Porter

When the little bluebird,
Who has never said a word,
Starts to sing "spring, spring"

When the little bluebell,
In the bottom of the dell,
Starts to ring: "ding, ding"

When the little blue clerk,
In the middle of his work,
Starts a tune to the moon up above,
It is nature, that's all,
Simply telling us to fall
In love.

And that's why
Birds do it, Bees do it,
Even educated fleas do it,
Let's do it, let's fall in love.
In Spain, the best upper sets do it,
Lithuanians and Let's do it,
Let's do it, let's fall in love.
The Dutch in old Amsterdam do it,
Not to mention the Finns,
Folks in Siam do it,
Think of Siamese twins.
Some Argentines, without means, do it,
People say, in Boston, even bean do it,
Let's do it, let's fall in love.

Romantic Sponges, they say, do it,
Oysters, down in Oyster Bay, do it,
Let's do it, let's fall in love.
Cold Cape Cod clams, 'gainst
their wish, do it,
Even lazy Jellyfish do it,
Let's do it, let's fall in love.
Electric eels, I might add, do it,
Though it shocks 'em I know.

Why ask if shad do it,
Waiter, bring me shad roe.
In shallow shoals, English soles do it,
Goldfish, in the privacy of bowls, do it,

Let's do it, let's fall in love.

Letters from Napoleon Bonaparte to his wife, Josephine

1797

I love you no longer; on the contrary, I detest you. You are a wretch, truly perverse, truly stupid, a real Cinderella. You never write to me at all, you do not love your husband; you know the pleasure that your letters give him yet you cannot even manage to write him half a dozen lines, dashed off in a moment! What then do you do all day, Madame? What business is so vital that it robs you of the time to write to your faithful lover? What attachment can be stifling and pushing aside the love, the tender and constant love, which you promised him? Who can this wonderful lover be who takes up your every moment, rules your days, and prevents you from devoting your attention to your husband? Beware, Josephine; one fine night the doors will be broken down and there I shall be.

April 8, 1796

I am not satisfied with your last letter: it is as cold as friendship.

June 16, 1796

You know quite well that I could not bear to let you have a lover, still less to offer you one. To tear out his heart and to see him would be the same thing for me.

Napoleon Bonaparte to his wife, Josephine

June 16, 1976

I openly admit I hate every one who is near you.

1796

You call me vous. Vous yourself!

1796

Woman!

French military genius Napoleon Bonaparte wed his wife Josephine Tascher de la Pagerie in 1796. They divorced in 1809 after 13 years together.

The Frog and the Mouse
Anonymous

A frog went walking one fine day
    A-hmmm, A-hmmm,
A frog went walking one fine day,
He met Miss Mousie on the way
    A-hmmm, A-hmmm.

He said Miss Mousie will you marry me,
    A-hmmm, A-hmmm,
He said Miss Mousie will you marry me,
We'll live together in a hollow tree,
    A-hmmm, A-hmmm.

The first to the wedding was farmer Brown
    A-hmmm, A-hmmm,
The first to the wedding was farmer Brown
He brought his wife in a wedding gown.
    A-hmmm, A-hmmm.

The second to the wedding was Dr. Dick
    A-hmmm, A-hmmm,
The second to the wedding was Dr. Dick
He ate so much that he nearly got sick.
    A-hmmm, A-hmmm.

The third to the wedding was Grandma Green
    A-hmmm, A-hmmm,
The third to the wedding was Grandma Green
Her shawl was blue but it wasn't clean.
    A-hmmm, A-hmmm.

And what do you think they had for supper?
    A-hmmm, A-hmmm,
And what do you think they had for supper?
Some fried mosquitoes without any butter.
    A-hmmm, A-hmmm.

And what do you think they had for a fiddle?
    A-hmmm, A-hmmm,
And what do you think they had for a fiddle?
An old tin can with a hole in the middle.
    A-hmmm, A-hmmm.

And what do you think they had on the shelf?
    A-hmmm, A-hmmm,
And what do you think they had on the shelf?
If you want to find out, go look for yourself!
    A-hmmm, A-hmmm.

The Aphrodisiac Dinner for Her

*F*oods are aphrodisiac because they have stimulating spices, sensuous tastes and textures, lush and evocative shapes. For a seductive dinner, flowers are also essential. A bouquet of red tulips or roses represents a declaration of true and passionate love. And don't forget candlelight. It's always flattering, and creates an intimate setting at your table.

Grilled Filet Mignon
Grilled Oysters
Polenta with Parmesan
Asparagus with Brown Butter
Strawberries & Sugared Grapes
Chocolates

1 egg white
1 box strawberries
1 bunch Thompson seedless grapes
package of polenta mix
coarse ground sea salt
coarse black pepper
1 bunch asparagus
3/4 cup parmesan cheese
6–8 oysters on the half shell
barbecue sauce (optional)
2 filet mignon steaks 2-inches thick

2 tablespoons butter
1/2 teaspoon dill weed
juice of 1/2 lime
11/2 cups superfine granulated sugar
2 top-of-the-line chocolate bars, or box
   of fine chocolates

Ahead of time...

1. Beat the egg white until bubbly, not foamy.
2. Wash the fruit, dry with paper towel.
3. Dip strawberries into superfine sugar, set aside.
4. Dip grapes into egg white, shaking off the excess; dust with superfine sugar, set on paper towel to dry.
5. Prepare polenta according to package instructions. (The microwave method is painless, no constant stirring.)

The Aphrodisiac Dinner for Her *(continued)*

6. Cover a saucer with a layer of coarse sea salt and cracked pepper and coat both sides and edges of the steaks.
7. Cut tough ends off asparagus, put into steamer (don't turn on yet).
8. Cover the bottom of a 9-inch pan with half the Parmesan cheese.
9. Pour hot polenta on the cheese, spread 1/2-inch thick.
10. Sprinkle with remaining Parmesan cheese, set aside.

Greet your woman with wine, then cook.

1. Heat your grill, or gas or charcoal barbecue.
2. Barbecue oysters 8–12 minutes with a dab of your favorite barbecue sauce, or a little butter.

Eat oysters, then...

1. Grill the steaks (in a gas or covered grill, usually 9–10 minutes on each side for medium, 10–12 minutes on each side for well done).
2. When steaks are done, cook asparagus 8–10 minutes, until they are tender when punctured with a fork, but not limp.
3. Cut the polenta into heart shapes with a cookie cutter.
4. Arrange sugared strawberries and grapes with chocolate on a pretty plate. Set aside.
5. Brown the butter in a frying pan, add dill and lime juice, toss asparagus to coat.

Serve dinner.

Thank You, My Dear

Sappho

Thank you, my dear

You came, and you did
well to come: I needed
you. You have made

love blaze up in
my breast—bless you!
Bless you as often

as the hours have
been endless to me
while you were gone

Camille

Alexandre Dumas

The room to which she had fled was lit only by a single candle. She lay back on a great sofa, her dress undone, holding one hand on her heart, and letting the other hang by her side. On the table was a basin half full of water, and the water was stained with streaks of blood.

Very pale, her mouth half open, Marguerite tried to recover breath. Now and again her bosom was raised by a long sigh, which seemed to relieve her a little, and for a few seconds she would seem to be quite comfortable.

I went up to her; she made no movement, and I sat down and took the hand which was lying on the sofa.

"Ah! it is you," she said, with a smile.

I must have looked greatly agitated, for she added:

"Are you unwell, too?"

"No, but you: do you still suffer?"

"Very little"; and she wiped off with her handkerchief the tears which the coughing had brought to her eyes; "I am used to it now."

"You are killing yourself, madame," I said to her in a moved voice. "I wish I were a friend, a relation of yours, that I might keep you from doing yourself harm like this."

"Ah! it is really not worth your while to alarm yourself," she replied in a somewhat bitter tone; "see how much notice the others take of me! They know too well that there is nothing to be done."

Thereupon she got up, and, taking the candle, put it on the mantel-piece and looked at herself in the glass.

"How pale I am!" she said, as she fastened her dress and passed her fingers over her loosened hair. "Come, let us go back to supper. Are you coming?"

I sat still and did not move.

She saw how deeply I had been affected by the whole scene, and, coming up to me, held out her hand, saying:

"Come now, let us go."

I took her hand, raised it to my lips, and in spite of myself two tears fell upon it.

"Why, what a child you are!" she said, sitting down by my side again. "You are crying! What is the matter?"

"I must seem very silly to you, but I am frightfully troubled by what I have just seen."

"You are very good! What would you have of me? I can not sleep. I must amuse myself a little. And then, girls like me, what does it matter, one more or less? The doctors tell me that the blood I spit up comes from my throat; I pretend to believe them; it is all I can do for them."

"Listen, Marguerite," I said, unable to contain myself any longer; "I do not know what influence you are going to have over my life, but at this present

The room to which she had fled was lit only by a single candle. She lay back on a great sofa, her dress undone, holding one hand on her heart, and letting the other hang by her side. On the table was a basin half full of water, and the water was stained with streaks of blood.

Very pale, her mouth half open, Marguerite tried to recover breath. Now and again her bosom was raised by a long sigh, which seemed to relieve her a little, and for a few seconds she would seem to be quite comfortable.

I went up to her; she made no movement, and I sat down and took the hand which was lying on the sofa.

"Ah! it is you," she said, with a smile.

I must have looked greatly agitated, for she added:

"Are you unwell, too?"

"No, but you: do you still suffer?"

"Very little"; and she wiped off with her handkerchief the tears which the coughing had brought to her eyes; "I am used to it now."

"You are killing yourself, madame," I said to her in a moved voice. "I wish I were a friend, a relation of yours, that I might keep you from doing yourself harm like this."

"Ah! it is really not worth your while to alarm yourself," she replied in a somewhat bitter tone; "see how much notice the others take of me! They know too well that there is nothing to be done."

Thereupon she got up, and, taking the candle, put it on the mantel-piece and looked at herself in the glass.

"How pale I am!" she said, as she fastened her dress and passed her fingers over her loosened hair. "Come, let us go back to supper. Are you coming?"

I sat still and did not move.

She saw how deeply I had been affected by the whole scene, and, coming up to

"And even all night?"

"As long as I did not weary you."

"And what do you call that?"

"Devotion."

"And what does this devotion come from?"

"The irresistible sympathy which I have for you."

"So you are in love with me? Say it straight out, it is much more simple."

"It is possible; but if I am to say it to you one day, it is not to-day."

"You will do better never to say it."

"Why?"

"Because only one of two things can come of it."

"What?"

"Either I shall not accept: then you will have a grudge against me; or I shall accept: then you will have a sorry mistress; a woman who is nervous, ill, sad, or gay with a gaiety sadder than grief, a woman who spits blood and spends a hundred thousand francs a year. That is all very well for a rich old man like the duke, but it is very bad for a young man like you, and the proof of it is that all the young lovers I have had have very soon left me."

I did not answer; I listened. This frankness, which was almost a kind of confession, the sad life, of which I caught some glimpse through the golden veil which covered it, and whose reality the poor girl sought to escape in dissipation, drink, and wakefulness, impressed me so deeply that I could not utter a single word.

"Come," continued Marguerite, "we are talking mere childishness. Give me your arm and let us go back to the dining-

228

room. They won't know what we mean by our absence."

"Go in, if you like, but allow me to stay here."

"Why?"

"Because your mirth hurts me."

"Well, I will be sad."

"Marguerite, let me say to you something which you have no doubt often heard, so often that the habit of hearing it has made you believe it no longer, but which is none the less real, and which I will never repeat."

"And that is . . . ?" she said, with the smile of a young mother listening to some foolish notion of her child.

"It is this, that ever since I have seen you, I know not why, you have taken a place in my life; that, if I drive the thought of you out of my mind, it always comes back; that when I met you to-day, after not having seen you for two years, you made a deeper impression on my heart and mind than ever; that, now that you have let me come to see you, now that I know you, now that I know all that is strange in you, you have become a necessity of my life, and you will drive me mad, not only if you will not love me, but if you will not let me love you."

"But, foolish creature that you are, I shall say to you, like Mme. D., 'You must be very rich, then!' Why, you don't know that I spend six or seven thousand francs a month, and that I could not live without it; you don't know, my poor friend, that I should ruin you in no time, and that your family would cast you off if you were to live with a woman like me. Let us be friends, good friends, but no more. Come and see me, we will laugh and talk, but don't exaggerate what I am worth, for I am worth very little. You have a good heart, you want some one to love you, you are too young and too sensitive to live in a world like mine.

229

Take a married woman. You see, I speak to you frankly, like a friend."

"But what the devil are you doing there?" cried Prudence, who had come in without our hearing her, and who now stood just inside the door with her hair half coming down and her dress undone. I recognized the hand of Gaston.

"We are talking sense," said Marguerite; "leave us alone; we will be back soon."

"Good, good! Talk, my children," said Prudence, going out and closing the door behind her, as if to further emphasize the tone in which she had said these words.

"Well, it is agreed," continued Marguerite, when we were alone, "you won't fall in love with me?"

"I will go away."

"So much as that?"

I had gone too far to draw back; and I was really carried away. This mingling of gaiety, sadness, candor, prostitution,

her very malady, which no doubt developed in her a sensitiveness to impressions, as well as an irritability of nerves, all this made it clear to me that if from the very beginning I did not completely dominate her light and forgetful nature, she was lost to me.

"Come, now, do you seriously mean what you say?" she said.

"Seriously."

"But why didn't you say it to me sooner?"

"When could I have said it?"

"The day after you had been introduced to me at the Opéra Comique."

"I thought you would have received me very badly if I had come to see you."

"Why?"

"Because I had behaved so stupidly."

"That's true. And yet you were already in love with me."

"Yes."

"And that didn't hinder you from

going to bed and sleeping quite comfortably. One knows what that sort of love means."

"There you are mistaken. Do you know what I did that evening, after the Opéra Comique?"

"No."

"I waited for you at the door of the Café Anglais. I followed the carriage in which you and your three friends were, and when I saw you were the only one to get down, and that you went in alone, I was vary happy."

Marguerite began to laugh.

"What are you laughing at?"

"Nothing."

"Tell me, I beg of you, or I shall think you are still laughing at me."

"You won't be cross?"

"What right have I to be cross?"

"Well, there was a sufficient reason why I went in alone."

"What?"

"Some one was waiting for me here."

If she had thrust a knife into me she would not have hurt me more. I rose, and holding out my hand, "Good-bye," said I.

"I knew you would be cross," she said; "men are frantic to know what is certain to give them pain."

"But I assure you," I added coldly, as if wishing to prove how completely I was cured of my passion, "I assure you that I am not cross. It was quite natural that some one should be waiting for you, just as it is quite natural that I should go from here at three in the morning."

"Have you, too, some one waiting for you?"

"No, but I must go."

"Good-bye, then."

"You send me away?"

"Not the least in the world."

"Why are you so unkind to me?"

"How have I been unkind to you?"

"In telling me that some one was waiting for you."

"I could not help laughing at the idea that you had been so happy to see me come in alone when there was such a good reason for it."

"One finds pleasure in childish enough things, and it is too bad to destroy such a pleasure when, by simply leaving it alone, one can make somebody so happy."

"But what do you think I am? I am neither maid nor duchess. I didn't know you till to-day, and I am not responsible to you for my actions. Supposing one day I should become your mistress, you are bound to know that I have had other lovers besides you. If you make scenes of jealousy like this before, what will it be like after, if that after should ever exist? I never met any one like you."

"That is because no one has ever loved you as I love you."

"Frankly, then, you really love me?"

"As much as it is possible to love, I think."

"And that has lasted since—?"

"Since the day I saw you go into Susse's, three years ago."

"Do you know, that is tremendously fine? Well, what am I to do in return?"

"Love me a little," I said, my heart beating so that I could hardly speak; for, in spite of the half-mocking smiles with which she had accompanied the whole conversation, it seemed to me that Marguerite began to share my agitation, and that the hour so long awaited was drawing near.

233

"Well, but the duke?"

"What duke?"

"My jealous old duke."

"He will know nothing."

"And if he should?"

"He would forgive you."

"Ah, no, he would leave me, and what would become of me?"

"You risk that for some one else."

"How do you know?"

"By the order you gave not to admit any one tonight."

"It is true; but that is a serious friend."

"For whom you care nothing, as you have shut your door against him at such an hour."

"It is not for you to reproach me, since it was in order to receive you, you and your friend."

Little by little I

had drawn nearer to Marguerite. I had put my arms about her waist, and I felt her supple body weigh lightly on my clasped hands.

"If you knew how much I love you!" I said in a low voice.

"Really true?"

"I swear it."

"Well, if you will promise to do everything I tell you, without a word, without an opinion, without a question, perhaps I will say yes."

"I will do everything that you wish!"

"But I forewarn you I must be free to do as I please, without giving you the slightest details what I do. I have long wished for a young

234

lover, who should be young and not self-willed, loving without distrust, loved without claiming the right to it. I have never found one. Men, instead of being satisfied in obtaining for a long time what they scarcely hoped to obtain once, exact from their mistresses a full account of the present, the past, and even the future. As they get accustomed to her, they want to rule her, and the more one gives them the more exacting they become. If I decide now on taking a new lover, he must have three very rare qualities: he must be confiding, submissive, and discreet."

"Well, I will be all that you wish."

"We shall see."

"When shall we see?"

"Later on."

"Why?"

"Because," said Marguerite, releasing herself from my arms, and taking from a great bunch of red camellias a single camellia, she placed it in my buttonhole, "because one can not always carry out agreements the day they are signed."

"And when shall I see you again?" I said, clasping her in my arms.

"When this camellia changes colour."

"When will it change colour?"

"To-morrow night between eleven and twelve. Are you satisfied?"

"Need you ask me?"

"Not a word of this either to your friend or to Prudence, or to anybody whatever."

"I promise."

"Now, kiss me, and we will go back to the dining-room."

She held up her lips to me, smoothed her hair again, and we went out of the room, she singing, and I almost beside myself.

I Watch You
Simon Ortiz

I watch you
from the gentle slope
where it is warm
by your shoulder.
My eyes are closed.
I can feel the tap
of your blood
against my cheek.
Inside my mind,
I see the gentle move
ment of your valleys,
the undulations
of slow turnings.

Opening my eyes,
there is a soft dark
and beautiful butte
moving up and down
as you breathe.
There are fine
and very tiny ferns
growing, and I can
make them move
by breathing.
I watch you with my skin
moving upon yours,
and I have known you well.

Notes between Rachel Felix and Prince de Joinville

TO RACHEL   *1840*

> Where?
> When?
> How Much?

TO THE PRINCE

> Your place.
> Tonight.
> Free.

Come, and Be My Baby
Maya Angelou

The highway is full of big cars going nowhere fast
And folks is smoking anything that'll burn
Some people wrap their lives around a cocktail glass
And you sit wondering
where you're going to turn
I got it.
Come. And be my baby.
Some prophets say the world is gonna end tomorrow
But others say we've got a week or two
The paper is full of every kind of blooming horror
And you sit wondering
What you're gonna do.
I got it.
Come. And be my baby.

*Letter from Franz Kafka
to Felice Bauer*

November 11, 1902

Write to me only once a week, so that your letter arrives on Sunday—for I cannot endure your daily letters. I am incapable of enduring them. For instance, I answer one of your letters, then lie in bed in apparent calm, but my heart beats through my entire body and is conscious only of you, I belong to you; there is really no other way of expressing it, and that is not strong enough. But for this very reason I don't want to know what you are wearing; it confuses me so much that I cannot deal with life.

*Austrian writer Franz Kafka proposed twice to Felice Bauer
after meeting her in 1912. Their relationship ended in
1917 with the breaking off of their second engagement.*

Luscious Lemon Hearts

These are tart and sweet at the same time and if you use heart cookie cutters, they couldn't be more perfect for any romantic occasion. This recipe makes about 36 2-inch squares or hearts, depending on the size of your cookie cutter.

CRUST
    3 1/2 cups all-purpose white flour
    1/4 cup confectioners' sugar
    1/4 teaspoon salt
    28 tablespoons (3 1/2 sticks) unsalted
        butter, cut into bits

1. Preheat the oven to 350°F.
2. In a large bowl, sift together the flour, sugar, and salt. With a pastry blender or two knives, cut the butter into the flour mixture until it has the consistency of cornmeal.
3. Press the dough onto a large baking sheet (10 x 15-inch, with 2-inch high sides).
4. Bake for 20 minutes.

FILLING
    6 large eggs
    3 cups granulated sugar
    2 tablespoons grated lemon zest
    3/4 cup lemon juice
    2/3 cup all-purpose white flour
    1 teaspoon baking powder
    confectioners' sugar for dusting

1. While the crust is baking, beat the eggs until blended and then beat in the following ingredients slowly, in this order: sugar, lemon zest, lemon juice, flour/baking powder. Blend until smooth.
2. Pour the mixture over the crust and bake for 25 more minutes.
3. Cool in the pan set up on a rack. Using a sharp knife, carefully cut into squares or cut out with a deep heart cookie cutter and dust with confectioners' sugar.

My Mistress' Eyes Are Nothing Like the Sun

William Shakespeare

My mistress' eyes are nothing like the sun;
Coral is far more red than her lips' red:
If snow be white, why then her breasts are dun;
If hairs be wires, black wires grow on her head.
I have seen roses damaskt, red and white,
But no such roses see I in her cheeks;
And in some perfumes is there more delight
Than in the breath that from my mistress reeks.
I love to hear her speak, yet well I know
That music hath a far more pleasing sound;
I grant I never saw a goddess go;
My mistress, when she walks, treads on the ground.
    And yet, by heaven, I think my love as rare
    As any she belied with false compare.

The Wings of the Dove

Henry James

At this point Kate ceased to attend. He saw after a little that she had been following some thought of her own, and he had been feeling the growth of something determinant even through the extravagance of much of the pleasantry, the warm transparent irony, into which their livelier intimacy kept plunging like a confident swimmer. Suddenly she said to him with extraordinary beauty: "I engage myself to you for ever."

The beauty was in everything, and he could have separated nothing—couldn t have thought of her face as distinct from the whole joy. Yet her face had a new light. "And I pledge you—I call God to witness!—every spark of my faith; I give you every drop of my life." That was all, for the moment, but it was enough, and it was almost as quiet as if it were nothing. They were in the open air, in an alley of the Gardens; the great space, which seemed to arch just then higher and spread wider for them, threw them back into deep concentration. They moved by a common instinct to a spot, within sight, that struck them as fairly sequestered, and there, before their time together was spent, they had extorted from concentration every advance it could make them. They had exchanged vows and tokens, sealed their rich compact, solemnised, so far as breathed words and murmured sounds and lighted eyes and clasped hands could do it, their agreement to belong only, and to belong tremendously, to each other.

Letters between Charles Kingsley and his wife, Fanny

TO FANNY   October 1843

Darling, one resolution I made in my sorrow, that I would ask a boon of you and I wish to show you and my God that I have gained purity and self-control, that intense though my love is for your body, I do not love it but as an expression of your soul. And therefore, when we are married, will you consent to remain for the first month in my arms a virgin bride, a sister only? . . . Will not these thoughts give us more perfect delight when we lie naked in each other's arms, clasped together toying with each other's limbs, buried in each other's bodies, struggling, panting, dying for a moment. Shall we not feel then, even then, that there is more in store for us, that those thrilling writhings are but dim shadows of a union which shall be perfect?

Charles and Fanny Kingsley

TO CHARLES   30 December 1843

After dinner I shall perhaps feel worn out so I shall just lie on your bosom and say nothing but feel a great deal, and you will be very loving and call me your poor child. And then you will perhaps show me your Life of St Elizabeth, your wedding gift. And then after tea we will go up to rest! We will undress and bathe and then you will come to my room, and we will kiss and love very much and read psalms aloud together, and then we will kneel down and pray in our night dresses. Oh! What solemn bliss! How hallowing! And then you will take me up in your arms, will you not? And lay me down in bed. And then you will extinguish our light and come to me! How I will open my arms to you and then sink into yours! And you will kiss me and clasp me and we will both praise God alone in the dark night with His eye shining down upon us and His love enclosing us. After a time we shall sleep!

Charles and Fanny Kingsley

And yet I fear you will yearn so for fuller communion that you will not be so happy as me. And I too perhaps shall yearn, frightened as I am! But every yearning will remind me of our self-denial, your sorrow for sin, your strength of repentance. And I shall glory in my yearning, please God!

TO FANNY   24 July 1857

Oh that I were with you, or rather you with me here. The beds are so small that we should be forced to lie inside each other, and the weather is so hot that you might walk about naked all day, as well as night—cela va sans dire! Oh, those naked nights at Chelsea! When will they come again? I kiss both locks of hair every time I open my desk—but the little curly one seems to bring me nearer to you.

Charles Kingsley, preacher and canon at Westminister Abbey, first courted his wife, Fanny, in the summer of 1839. After a four-year courtship, they were married at Trinity Church in Bath on January 10, 1844. They were together until he died in 1875.

259

Nuptial Sleep
Dante Gabriel Rossetti

At length their long kiss severed, with sweet smart:
    And as the last slow sudden drops are shed
    From sparkling eaves when all the storm has fled,
So singly flagged the pulses of each heart.
Their bosoms sundered, with the opening start
    Of married flowers to either side outspread
    From the knit stem; yet still their mouths, burnt red,
Fawned on each other where they lay apart.

Sleep sank them lower than the tide of dreams,
    And their dreams watched them sink, and slid away.
Slowly their souls swam up again, through gleams
    Of watered light and dull drowned waifs of day;
Till from some wonder of new woods and streams
    He woke, and wondered more: for there she lay.

Love Is Here To Stay

George Gershwin and Ira Gershwin

The more I read the papers
The less I comprehend
The world and all its capers
And how it all will end.
Nothing seems to be lasting,
But that isn't our affair;
We've got something permanent,
I mean in the way we care.

It's very clear
Our love is here to stay;
Not for a year
But ever and a day.

The radio and the telephone and
   the movies that we know
May just be passing fancies,
And in time may go.

But, oh my dear,
Our love is here to stay;
Together we're
Going a long, long way.
In time the Rockies may crumble,
Gibraltar may tumble,
They're only made of clay,
But our love is here to stay.

The Ultimate Chocolate Mousse

*T*his is beautiful and delicious and can be prepared well ahead of time. It can be served together with the lemon squares or with berries and whipped cream for a larger crowd. Makes 6–8 servings.

6 oz. (3 2-oz. squares) really good semi-sweet chocolate, finely chopped
4 eggs
2 teaspoons granulated sugar
1/4 cup strong espresso
2 tablespoons dark rum (if desired)
stainless steel mixing bowl, kept in freezer 1 hour
1 cup (approximately 1/2 pint) very cold heavy whipping cream
1 teaspoon sugar

1. Melt chocolate in double boiler.
2. Separate the eggs. Put yolks in a bowl together with the sugar and beat until they become pale yellow and creamy. Add the melted chocolate, coffee, and rum and mix them in with a wooden spoon until uniformly combined.
3. Take mixing bowl from freezer and add cream and 1 teaspoon sugar. Beat until they form high peaks, then fold into the chocolate/egg mixture.
4. In the now-empty mixing bowl, whip the egg whites until they form stiff peaks; then fold gently but thoroughly into chocolate mousse mixture.
5. Spoon the mousse into individual serving cups or one large bowl, cover with plastic wrap, and refrigerate overnight.
6. Serve with whipped cream or raspberries, or both.

Cupid and Psyche

Thomas Bulfinch

A certain king and queen had three daughters. The charms of the two elder were more than common, but the beauty of the youngest was so wonderful that the poverty of language is unable to express its due praise. The fame of her beauty was so great that strangers from neighboring countries came in crowds to enjoy the sight, and looked on her with amazement, paying her that homage which is due only to Venus herself. In fact Venus found her altars deserted, while men turned their devotion to this young virgin. As she passed along, the people sang her praises and strewed her way with chaplets and flowers.

This perversion of homage due only to the immortal powers to the exaltation of a mortal gave great offense to the real Venus. Shaking her ambrosial locks with indignation, she exclaimed, "Am I then to be eclipsed in my honors by a mortal girl? In vain then did that royal shepherd, whose judgment was approved by Jove himself, give me the palm of beauty over my illustrious rivals, Pallas and Juno. But she shall not so quietly usurp my honors. I will give her cause to repent of so unlawful a beauty."

Thereupon she calls her winged son Cupid, mischievous enough in his own nature, and rouses and provokes him yet more by her complaints. She points out Psyche to him and says, "My dear son, punish that contumacious beauty; give thy mother a revenge as sweet as her injuries are great; infuse into the bosom of that haughty girl a passion for some low, mean, unworthy being, so that she may reap a mortification as great as her present exultation and triumph."

Cupid prepared to obey the commands of his mother. There are two fountains in Venus's garden, one of sweet waters, the other of bitter. Cupid filled two amber vases, one from each fountain, and suspending them from the top of his quiver, hastened to the chamber of Psyche, whom he found asleep. He shed a few drops from the bitter fountain over her lips, though the sight of her almost moved him to pity; then touched her side with the point of his arrow. At the touch she awoke, and opened eyes upon Cupid (himself invisible), which so startled him that in his confusion he wounded himself with his own arrow. Heedless of his wound his whole thought was to repair the mischief he had done, and he poured the balmy drops of joy over all her silken ringlets.

Psyche, henceforth frowned upon by Venus, derived no benefit from all her charms. True, all eyes were cast eagerly upon her, and every mouth spoke her praises; but neither king, royal youth, nor plebeian presented himself to demand her in marriage. Her two elder sisters of moderate charms had now long been married to two royal princes; but Psyche, in her lonely apartment, deplored her solitude, sick of that beauty which, while it procured abundance of flattery, had failed to awaken love.

Her parents, afraid that they had unwittingly incurred the anger of the gods, consulted the oracle of Apollo and received this answer: "The virgin is destined for the bride of no mortal lover. Her future husband awaits her on the top of the mountain. He is a monster whom neither gods nor men can resist."

This dreadful decree of the oracle filled all the people with dismay, and her parents abandoned themselves to grief. But Psyche said, "Why, my dear parents, do you now lament me? You should rather have grieved when the people showered upon me undeserved honors and with one voice called me a Venus. I

now perceive that I am a victim to that name. I submit. Lead me to that rock to which my unhappy fate has destined me." Accordingly, all things being prepared, the royal maid took her place in the procession, which more resembled a funeral than a nuptial pomp, and with her parents, amid the lamentations of the people, ascended the mountain, on the summit of which they left her alone, and with sorrowful hearts returned home.

While Psyche stood on the ridge of the mountain, panting with fear and with eyes full of tears, the gentle Zephyr raised her from the earth and bore her with an easy motion into a flowery dale. By degrees her mind became composed, and she laid herself down on the grassy bank to sleep. When she awoke refreshed with sleep, she looked round and beheld near by a pleasant grove of tall and stately

trees. She entered it, and in the midst discovered a fountain, sending forth clear and crystal waters, and fast by, a magnificent palace whose august front impressed the spectator that it was not the work of mortal hands, but the happy retreat of some god. Drawn by admiration and wonder, she approached the building and ventured to enter. Every object she met filled her with pleasure and amazement. Golden pillars supported the vaulted roof, and the walls were enriched with carvings and paintings representing beasts of the chase and rural scenes, adapted to delight the eye of the beholder. Proceeding onward, she perceived that besides the apartments of state there were others filled with all manner of treasures, and beautiful and precious productions of nature and art.

While her eyes were thus occupied, a voice addressed her, though she saw no one, uttering these words: "Sovereign lady, all that you see is yours. We whose voices you hear are your servants and shall obey all your commands with our utmost care and diligence. Retire therefore to your chamber and repose on your bed of down, and when you see fit, repair to the bath. Supper awaits you in the adjoining alcove when it pleases you to take your seat there."

Psyche gave ear to the admonitions of her vocal attendants, and after repose and the refreshment of the bath, seated herself in the alcove, where a table immediately presented itself, without any visible aid from waiters or servants, and covered with the greatest delicacies of food and the most nectareous wines. Her ears too were feasted with music from invisible performers; of whom one sang, another played on the lute, and all closed in the wonderful harmony of a full chorus.

She had not yet seen her destined husband. He came only in the hours of darkness and fled before the dawn of morning, but his accents were full of love and inspired a like passion in her. She often begged him to stay and let her behold him, but he would not consent. On the contrary he charged her to make no attempt to see him, for it was his pleasure, for the best of reasons, to keep concealed. "Why should you wish to behold me?" he said; "have you any doubt of my love? Have you any wish ungratified? If you saw me, perhaps you would fear me, perhaps adore me, but all I ask of you is to love me. I would rather you would love me as an equal than adore me as a god."

This reasoning somewhat quieted Psyche for a time, and while the novelty lasted she felt quite happy. But at length the thought of her parents, left in ignorance of her fate, and of her sisters, precluded from sharing with her the delights of her situation, preyed on her mind and made her begin to feel her palace as but a splendid prison. When her husband came one night, she told him her distress, and at last drew from him an unwilling consent that her sisters should be brought to see her.

So calling Zephyr, she acquainted him with her husband's commands, and he, promptly obedient, soon brought them across the mountain down to their sister's valley. They embraced her and she returned their caresses. "Come," said Psyche, "enter with me my house and refresh yourselves with whatever your sister has to offer." Then taking their hands she led them into her golden palace, and committed them to the care of her numerous train of attendant

273

voices, to refresh them in her baths and at her table and to show them all her treasures. The view of these celestial delights caused envy to enter their bosoms, at seeing their young sister possessed of such state and splendor, so much exceeding their own.

They asked her numberless questions, among others what sort of person her husband was. Psyche replied that he was a beautiful youth, who generally spent the daytime in hunting upon the mountains. The sisters, not satisfied with this reply, soon made her confess that she had never seen him. Then they proceeded to fill her bosom with dark suspicions. "Call to mind," they said, "the Pythian oracles that declared you destined to marry a direful and tremendous monster. The inhabitants of this valley say that your husband is a terrible and monstrous serpent, who nourishes you for a while with dainties that he may by and by devour

you. Take our advice. Provide yourself with a lamp and a sharp knife; put them in concealment that your husband may not discover them, and when he is sound asleep, slip out of bed, bring forth your lamp and see for yourself whether what they say is true or not. If it is, hesitate not to cut off the monster's head and thereby recover your liberty."

Psyche resisted these persuasions as well as she could, but they did not fail to have their effect on her mind, and when her sisters were gone, their words and her own curiosity were too strong for her to resist. So she prepared her lamp and a sharp knife and hid them out of sight of her husband. When he had fallen into his first sleep, she silently rose and uncovering her lamp beheld not a hideous monster, but the most beautiful and charming of the gods, with his golden ringlets wandering over his snowy neck and crimson cheek, with two dewy wings

274

on his shoulders, whiter than snow, and with shining feathers like the tender blossoms of spring. As she leaned the lamp over to have a nearer view of his face a drop of burning oil fell on the shoulder of the god, startled with which he opened his eyes and fixed them full upon her; then, without saying one word, he spread his white wings and flew out of the window. Psyche, in vain endeavoring to follow him, fell from the window to the ground. Cupid, beholding her as she lay in the dust, stopped his flight for an instant and said, "O foolish Psyche, is it thus you repay my love? After having disobeyed my mother's commands and made you my wife, will you think me a monster and cut off my head? But go; return to your sisters, whose advice you seem to think preferable to mine. I inflict no other punishment on you than to leave you forever. Love cannot dwell with suspicion." So saying, he fled away, leaving poor Psyche prostrate on the ground, filling the place with mournful lamentations.

When she had recovered some degree of composure she looked around her, but the palace and gardens had vanished, and she found herself in the open field not far from the city where her sisters dwelt. She repaired thither and told them the whole story of her misfortunes, at which, pretending to grieve, those spiteful creatures inwardly rejoiced; "For now," said they, "he will perhaps choose one of us." With this idea, without saying a word of her intentions, each of them rose early the next morning and ascended the mountain, and having reached the top, called upon Zephyr to receive her and bear her to his lord; then

leaping up, and not being sustained by Zephyr, fell down the precipice and was dashed to pieces.

Psyche, meanwhile, wandered day and night, without food or repose, in search of her husband. Casting her eyes on a lofty mountain having on its brow a magnificent temple, she sighed and said to herself, "Perhaps my love, my lord, inhabits there," and directed her steps thither.

She had no sooner entered than she saw heaps of corn, some in loose ears and some in sheaves, with mingled ears of barley. Scattered about lay sickles and rakes and all the instruments of harvest, without order, as if thrown carelessly out of the weary reapers' hands in the sultry hours of the day.

This unseemly confusion the pious Psyche put an end to, by separating and sorting every thing to its proper place and kind, believing that she ought to neglect none of the gods, but endeavor by her piety to engage them all in her behalf. The holy Ceres, whose temple it was, finding her so religiously employed, thus spoke to her: "Oh Psyche, truly worthy of our pity, though I cannot shield you from the frowns of Venus, yet I can teach you how best to allay her displeasure. Go then and voluntarily surrender yourself to your lady and sovereign, and try by modesty and submission to win her forgiveness, and perhaps her favor will restore you the husband you have lost."

Psyche obeyed the commands of Ceres and took her way to the temple of Venus, endeavoring to fortify her mind and ruminating on what she should say and how best propitiate the angry goddess, feeling that the issue was doubtful and perhaps fatal.

Venus received her with angry countenance. "Most undutiful and faithless of

277

servants," said she, "do you at last remember that you really have a mistress? Or have you rather come to see your sick husband, yet laid up of the wound given him by his loving wife? You are so ill favored and disagreeable that the only way you can merit your lover must be by dint of industry and diligence. I will make trial of your housewifery." Then she ordered Psyche to be led to the storehouse of her temple, where was laid up a great quantity of wheat, barley, millet, vetches, beans, and lentils prepared for food for her pigeons, and said, "Take and separate all these grains, putting all of the same kind in a parcel by themselves, and see that you get it done before evening." Then Venus departed and left her to her task.

But Psyche, in a perfect consternation at the enormous work, sat stupid and silent, without moving a finger to the inextricable heap.

While she sat despairing Cupid stirred up the little ant, a native of the fields, to take compassion on her. The leader of the ant hill, followed by whole hosts of his six-legged subjects, approached the heap, and with the utmost diligence taking grain by grain, they separated the pile, sorting each kind to its parcel; and when it was all done, they vanished out of sight in a moment.

Venus at the approach of twilight returned from the banquet of the gods, breathing odors and crowned with roses. Seeing the task done, she exclaimed, "This is no work of yours, wicked one, but his, whom to your own and his misfortune you have enticed." So saying, she threw her a piece of black bread for her supper and went away.

Next morning Venus ordered Psyche

to be called and said to her, "Behold yonder grove which stretches along the margin of the water. There you will find sheep feeding without a shepherd, with golden-shining fleeces on their backs. Go, fetch me a sample of that precious wool gathered from every one of their fleeces."

Psyche obediently went to the river-side, prepared to do her best to execute the command. But the river god inspired the reeds with harmonious murmurs, which seemed to say, "Oh, maiden, severely tried, tempt not the dangerous flood, nor venture among the formidable rams on the other side, for as long as they are under the influence of the rising sun, they burn with a cruel rage to destroy mortals with their sharp horns or rude teeth. But when the noontide sun has driven the cattle to the shade, and the serene spirit of the flood has lulled them to rest, you may then cross in safe-ty, and you will find the woolly gold sticking to the bushes and the trunks of the trees."

Thus the compassionate river god gave Psyche instructions how to accomplish her task, and by observing his directions she soon returned to Venus with her arms full of the golden fleece; but she received not the approbation of her implacable mistress, who said, "I know very well it is by none of your own doings that you have succeeded in this task, and I am not satisfied yet that you have any capacity to make yourself use-ful. But I have another task for you. Here, take this box, and go your way to the infernal shades, and give this box to Proserpine and say, 'My mistress Venus desires you to send her a little of your beauty, for in tending her sick son she has lost some of her own.' Be not too long on your errand, for I must paint myself with it to appear at the circle of the gods and goddesses this evening."

279

Psyche was now satisfied that her destruction was at hand, being obliged to go with her own feet directly down to Erebus. Wherefore, to make no delay of what was not to be avoided, she goes to the top of a high tower to precipitate herself headlong, thus to descend the shortest way to the shades below. But a voice from the tower said to her, "Why, poor unlucky girl, dost thou design to put an end to thy days in so dreadful a manner? And what cowardice makes thee sink under this last danger who hast been so miraculously supported in all thy former?" Then the voice told her how by a certain cave she might reach the realms of Pluto, and how to avoid all the dangers of the road, to pass by Cerberus, the three-headed dog, and prevail on Charon, the ferryman, to take her across the black river and bring her back again. But the voice added, "When Proserpine has given you the box, filled with her beauty, of all things this is chiefly to be observed by you, that you never once open or look into the box nor allow your curiosity to pry into the treasure of the beauty of the goddesses."

Psyche, encouraged by this advice obeyed it in all things, and taking heed to her ways travelled safely to the kingdom of Pluto. She was admitted to the palace of Proserpine, and without accepting the delicate seat or delicious banquet that was offered her, but contented with coarse bread for her food, she delivered her message from Venus. Presently the box was returned to her, shut and filled with the precious commodity. Then she returned the way she came, and glad was she to come out once more into the light of day.

But having got so far successfully through her dangerous task a longing desire seized her to examine the contents of the box. "What," said she, "shall I, the carrier of this divine beauty, not take the least bit to put on my cheeks to appear to more advantage in the eyes of my beloved husband!" So she carefully opened the box, but found nothing there of any beauty at all, but an infernal and truly Stygian sleep, which being thus set free from its prison, took possession of her, and she fell down in the midst of the road, a sleepy corpse without sense or motion.

But, Cupid, being now recovered from his wound, and not able longer to bear the absence of his beloved Psyche, slipping through the smallest crack of the window of his chamber which happened to be left open, flew to the spot where Psyche lay, and gathering up the sleep from her body closed it again in the box,

and waked Psyche with a light touch of one of his arrows. "Again," said he, "hast thou almost perished by the same curiosity. But now perform exactly the task imposed on you by my mother, and I will take care of the rest."

Then Cupid, as swift as lightning penetrating the heights of heaven, presented himself before Jupiter with his supplication. Jupiter lent a favoring ear and pleaded the cause of the lovers so earnestly with Venus that he won her consent. On this he sent Mercury to bring Psyche up to the heavenly assembly, and when she arrived, handing her a cup of ambrosia, he said, "Drink this, Psyche, and be immortal; nor shall Cupid ever break away from the knot in which he is tied, but these nuptials shall be perpetual."

Thus Psyche became at last united to Cupid, and in due time they had a daughter born to them whose name was Pleasure.

The Telephone
Robert Frost

"When I was just as far as I could walk
From here today,
There was an hour
All still
When leaning with my head against a flower
I heard you talk.
Don't say I didn't, for I heard you say—
You spoke from that flower on the window sill—
Do you remember what it was you said?"

"First tell me what it was you thought you heard."

"Having found the flower and driven a bee away,
I leaned my head,
And holding by the stalk,
I listened and I thought I caught the word—
What was it? Did you call me by my name?
Or did you say—
Someone said 'Come'—I heard it as I bowed."

"I may have thought as much, but not aloud."

"Well, so I came."

A poem from E. B. White to his wife, Katharine

Natural History

The spider, dropping down from twig,
Unwinds a thread of her devising:
A thin, premeditated rig
To use in rising.

And all the journey down through space,
In cool descent, and loyal-hearted,
She builds a ladder to the place
from which she started.

Thus I, gone forth, as spiders do,
In spider's web a truth discerning,
Attach one silken strand to you
for my returning.

American journalist and novelist Elwyn Brooks White married his boss and fellow journalist at The New Yorker magazine, Katharine Angell, on November 13, 1929. They were happily married for 48 years.

Letter from Sarah Bernhardt to Jean Richepin

1883

Carry me off into the blue skies of tender loves, roll me in dark clouds, tramp me with your thunderstorms, break me in your angry rages. But love me, my adored love.

Sarah Bernhardt, French actress, met Jean Richepin, French writer, when she agreed to produce his play, "La Glu," in the fall of 1883. Their relationship continued for the span of her career and ended with a final script commission in 1916.

Let Me Not to the Marriage of True Minds

William Shakespeare

Let me not to the marriage of true minds
Admit impediments; love is not love
Which alters when it alteration finds,
Or bends with the remover to remove.
O, no, it is an ever-fixed mark
That looks on tempests and is never shaken;
It is the star to every wand'ring bark,
Whose worth's unknown, although his height be taken.
Love's not Time's fool, though rosy lips and cheeks
Within his bending sickle's compass come;
Love alters not with his brief hours and weeks,
But bears it out even to the edge of doom.
    If this be error and upon me proved,
    I never writ, nor no man ever loved.

These Twain

Arnold Bennett

Now and then she was so bewildered by discoveries that she came to wonder why she had married him, and why people do marry—really! The fact was that she had married him for the look in his eyes. It was a sad look, and beyond that it could not be described. Also, a little, she had married him for his bright untidy hair, and for that short oblique shake of the head which, with him, meant a greeting or an affirmative. She had not married him for his sentiments nor for his goodness of heart. Some points in him she did not like. He had a tendency to colds, and she hated him whenever he had a cold. She often detested his terrible tidiness, though it was a convenient failing . . . . She did not like his way of walking, which was ungainly, nor his way of standing, which was infirm. She preferred him to be seated. She could not but regret his irresolution and his love of ease. However, the look in his eyes was paramount, because she was in love with him. She knew that he was more deeply and helplessly in love with her than she was with him, but even she was perhaps tightlier bound than in her pride she thought.

*Letter from Thomas Woodrow Wilson
to his wife, Ellen*

May 9, 1886

. . . I've been reckoning up, in a tumultuous, heartful sort of way, the value of my little wife to me. I can't state the result—there are no terms of value in which it can be stated—but perhaps I can give you some idea of what its proportions would be if it were stated. She has taken all real pain out of my life: her wonderful loving sympathy exalts even my occasional moods of despondency into a sort of hallowed sadness out of which I come stronger and better. She has given to my ambitions a meaning, an assurance, and a purity which they never had before: with her by my side, ardently devoted to me and to my cause, understanding all my thoughts and all my aims, I feel that I can make the utmost of every power I possess. She has brought into my life the sunshine which was needed to keep it from growing stale and morbid: that has steadily been bringing back into my spirits their old gladness and boyhood, their old delight

Thomas Woodrow Wilson to his wife, Ellen

in play and laughter: —that sweetest sunshine of deep, womanly love, unfailing, gentle patience, even happy spirits, and spontaneous mirth, that is purest, swiftest tonic to a spirit prone to fret and apt to flag. She has given me that perfect rest of heart and mind of whose existence I had never so much as dreamed before she came to me, which springs out of assured oneness of hope and sympathy—and which, for me, means life and success. Above all she has given me herself to live for! Her arms are able to hold me up against the world: her eyes are able to charm away every care; her words are my solace and inspiration and all because her love is my life...

Thomas Woodrow Wilson, twenty-eighth president of the United States, married his wife, Ellen Axson Wilson, on June 24, 1885. They were happily married for 29 years.

297

Such Different Wants

Robert Bly

The board floats on the river.
The board wants nothing
but is pulled from beneath
on into deeper waters.

And the elephant dwelling
on the mountain wants
a trumpet so its dying cry
can be heard by the stars.

The wakeful heron striding
through reeds at dawn wants
the god of sun and moon
to see his long skinny neck.

You must say what you want.
I want to be the man
and I am who will love you
when your hair is white.

Divine Tiramisu

*T*his is the Italian dessert that no restaurant makes the same but everyone loves no matter how it is made. Here is the easiest version to make at home. It serves 8 and, with a few strawberries on the side, makes a heavenly dessert for a Valentine dinner with your favorite couples.

2 cups (16 oz.) mascarpone (Italian cream cheese), at room temperature

1/2 cup confectioners' sugar

1 cup (approximately 1/2 pint) heavy whipping cream, chilled

1 teaspoon vanilla extract

1 1/2 cups cool, brewed espresso coffee, or 1 tablespoon instant espresso dissolved in 1 1/2 cups boiling water and then cooled

1/2 cup sweet marsala (you can substitute dark rum)

1 (7 oz.) package Italian dry ladyfingers (biscotti di savoiardi)

1–3 ounces dark bittersweet chocolate

1. Blend the mascarpone and sugar together until smooth.

2. Whip the cream with the vanilla extract until peaks form.

3. Fold the whipped cream and mascarpone together.

4. Mix the espresso and liquor together in a shallow dish.

5. Take half of the ladyfingers and dip them briefly (on both sides) in the espresso.

6. Arrange them in a single layer on a 7 x 11-inch serving dish and spread with half the mascarpone mixture.

7. Add a second layer and spread with the remaining mascarpone.

8. Cover tightly with plastic wrap and chill for at least 4 hours. Overnight is fine, too.

9. When you are ready to serve, using the coarse holes of a cheese grater, grate the chocolate and sprinkle over the top. If you don't have a chunk of bittersweet chocolate, you can also use unsweetened cocoa powder.

Letter from Tsarina Alexandra to her husband, Tsar Nicholas II of Russia

December 30, 1915

Off you go again alone & it's with a very heavy heart I part from you. No more kisses and tender caresses for ever so long—I want to bury myself into you, hold you tight in my arms, make you feel the intense love of mine. You are my very life Sweetheart, and every separation gives such endless heartache. . . . Goodbye my Angel, Husband of my heart I envy my flowers that will accompany you. I press you tightly to my breast, kiss every sweet place with gentle tender love. . . God bless and protect you, guard you from all harm, guide you safely & firmly into the new year. May it bring glory & sure peace, & the reward for all this war has cost you. I gently press my lips to yours & try to forget everything, gazing into your lovely eyes—I lay on your precious breast, rested my tired head upon it still. This morning I tried to gain calm & strength for the separation. Goodbye wee one, Lovebird, Sunshine, Huzy mine, Own!

Alexandra and Nicholas, future Tsarina and Tsar of Russia married on November 14, 1894. Their entire family was executed during the Communist Revolution in 1918.

Anna Karenina

Leo Tolstoy

When everyone was getting up from the table Levin wanted to follow Kitty into the drawing room, but he was afraid she might not like it if his attentions became too obvious. He stayed on with the group of men, taking part in the general conversation; without looking at Kitty he was aware of her movements, her looks, and where she was sitting.

Without the slightest effort he had begun at once to keep the promise he had made her—always to esteem and to love everyone. The conversation had gone on to the village commune, in which Pestsov saw some sort of special principle that he called the "choral" principle. Levin disagreed both with Pestsov and with his brother, Koznyshov, who in his usual way both admitted and didn't admit the significance of the Russian commune. But he spoke to them simply in an attempt to bring them together and soften their differences. He didn't have the slightest interest in what he was saying himself, and still less in what they were saying; all he wanted was for them and everyone else to be in a pleasant, cheerful mood.

He now knew the one thing that was important. And this one thing was there, at first in the drawing room, though then it began moving about and came to a stop in the doorway. Without turning around he felt a gaze directed at him and a smile, and he could not help turning around. She was standing in the doorway with Shcherbatsky looking at him.

"I thought you were going over to the piano," he said, moving toward her. "That's what I don't get enough of in the country—music."

"No, we only came over to call you away; thank you for coming," she said, rewarding him with her smile, as though it were a present. "What's the good of arguing? After all, no one ever convinces anyone else."

"That's true," said Levin, "what happens most of the time is that the only reason you argue so heatedly is because you simply can't make out just what your opponent is trying to prove."

Levin had often noticed, in arguments between the cleverest people, that after enormous efforts, and an enormous number of logical subtleties and words, the people who were arguing finally became aware that what they had been taking such pains to prove to each other had long since been known to them, from the very beginning of the argument on, but that they liked different things, and didn't want to mention what they liked in order not to be attacked. He had often had the experience in the midst of an argument of understanding what his opponent liked; he would suddenly get to like it himself and immediately agree, whereupon all arguments fell away, superfluous; sometimes he had the contrary experience: you finally said what it was you liked your self and why you had been thinking up arguments, and if you happened to express this well and sincerely, then your opponent would suddenly agree with you and stop arguing. He tried to say this now.

She wrinkled her forehead, trying to understand. But the moment he started explaining she had grasped it.

"I see—you have to find out what he's arguing in favor of, what he likes, then you can . . . ."

She had completely grasped his badly expressed thought and put it in the right words. Levin smiled joyfully, he was so struck by this transition from the confused, verbose argument with his brother and Pestsov to this laconic, clear, almost wordless communication of the most complicated ideas.

Shcherbatsky left them, and Kitty, going over to a table set out for cards, sat down and taking up a piece of chalk began drawing divergent circles on the new green cloth.

They resumed the conversation started at dinner—about the emancipation of women and their occupations. Levin agreed with Dolly's opinion that a girl who didn't get married would find woman's work for herself in a family. He supported this with the remark that there wasn't a single family that could get along without women to help, and that there were and had to be nurses, either hired ones or relatives, in every family, rich or poor.

"No," said Kitty, blushing, but looking at him with her candid eyes all the more boldly, "a girl may be so situated that she can't enter into a family without humiliating herself, while she herself—"

He understood the allusion.

"Oh yes!" he said, "yes, yes, yes, you're right, you're right!"

And he grasped everything Pestsov had been trying to demonstrate at dinner about women's freedom, simply by seeing in Kitty's heart the fear of humiliation and of spinsterhood, and through loving her he sensed this fear and humiliation and abruptly abandoned all his own arguments.

A silence came over them. She was still drawing with the chalk on the table. Her eyes were glowing softly. Yielding to her mood he felt a constantly growing tension of happiness throughout her whole being.

"Oh—I've scribbled all over the table!" she said, putting down the chalk and moving as though she were about to get up.

How can I stay here alone, without her? he thought horrified, and took up the piece of chalk. "Don't go," he said, sitting down at the table. "I've been wanting to ask you something for a long time."

He looked straight into her tender, though frightened eyes.

"Ask me—please!"

"There," he said, and wrote down the initial letters: w, y, g, m, t, a, i, i, n, p, d, y, m, i, w, n, b, p, o, t, i, w, p, t ? These letters stood for: "When you gave me the

answer 'It is not possible,' did you mean it would never be possible, or that it wasn't possible then?"

There wasn't the slightest likelihood of her being able to guess this complicated sentence; but he looked at her as though his life depended on whether she would.

She looked at him gravely; then she leaned her puckered forehead on her hand and began reading. Occasionally she looked up at him, her look asking him: "Is it what I think it is?"

"I understand it," she said, blushing.

"What's this word?" he said, pointing to the n, which stood for "never."

"That means 'never,'" she said, "but that's not so!"

He quickly rubbed out what he had written, gave her the chalk and got up. She wrote: t, w, n, o, a, I, c, g, t.

Dolly was quite consoled for the grief her conversation with Karenin had given her when she saw these two figures:

Kitty with the piece of chalk in her hand, looking up at Levin with a timid happy smile, and his handsome figure leaning over the table, with his burning eyes fixed now on her and now on the table. Suddenly he was radiant: he had guessed it. What it meant was: "There was no other answer I could give then."

He looked at her questioningly, timidly.

"Only then?"

"Yes," her smile replied.

"And n-n-n-now?" he asked.

"Well, read this now. I'll tell you what I should like. Should like very much!" She wrote down these initial letters: I, l, y, t, f, a, f, w, h. That meant: "I'd like you to forget and forgive what happened."

He seized the chalk in his taut, trembling fingers, broke it, and wrote down the initial letters of the following: "There's nothing for me to forget or forgive, I haven't stopped loving you."

She looked at him with a smile that did not falter.

"I understand," she said in a whisper.

He sat down and wrote out a long sentence. She understood it all and without asking him whether she had it right took the chalk and replied immediately.

For a long time he could not understand what she had written, and he kept looking into her eyes. He was numb with happiness. He could not fill in the words she meant at all, but in her lovely eyes, radiant with happiness, he understood everything he had to know. He wrote down three letters; but before he had even finished writing she had already read it under his hand; she had finished it herself, and written down the answer: "Yes."

"Playing 'secretary'?" said the old Prince, coming over to them. "Come along now. We really ought to be going if we're to be in time for the theater."

Levin got up and saw Kitty to the door.

Everything had been said in their conversation: what had been said was that she loved him and would tell her father and mother, and that he would call in the morning.

Letter from Simone de Beauvoir to Jean-Paul Sartre

February 16, 1940

I'm altogether immersed in the happiness I derive from seeing you. Nothing else counts. I have you—little all-precious one, little beloved one—as much today as the day before yesterday when I could see you, and I'll have you till the day I die. After that, nothing of all that may happen to me really has any importance. Not only am I not sad, I'm even deeply happy and secure. Even the tenderest memories—of all your dear expressions, or your little arms cradling the pillow in the morning—aren't painful to me. I feel myself all enfolded and sustained by your love.

French intellectual Simone de Beauvoir shared a 51-year relationship with her chosen partner and fellow philosopher, Jean-Paul Sartre.

319

Variation
Federico García Lorca

That still pool of the air
under the branch of an echo.

That still pool of the water
under a frond of bright stars.

That still pool of your mouth
under a thicket of kisses.

Meringues with Strawberries

Fat free, although loaded with sugar, this is a marvelous summer dessert. You can use mixed berries, too. And you can serve it with whipped cream, or strawberry puree, or a berry flavored yogurt. Serves 4 larger portions or 6 smaller ones.

MERINGUES

    4 large egg whites
    pinch of salt
    1/4 teaspoon vanilla extract
    1 cup sugar

1. Lay a sheet of parchment paper on top of your baking sheet. Preheat the oven to 250°F.
2. Beat the egg whites with the salt and vanilla until they hold soft peaks.
3. Add the sugar slowly, one tablespoon at a time, blending each one before moving on to the next. Keep whipping until the meringue is white, stiff, and shiny.
4. One large spoonful at a time, put 4 (or 6 if you are serving 6) big blobs of meringue, well separated, onto the parchment paper on your baking sheet. Add a second, then a third spoonful on top of your first. Now start shaping your mounds into circles and start moving what is in the center to the outer edges, so you are making little walls. As you keep adding what is left of the meringue, continue shaping until you have four little bowls. (The objective is to have a place to put the berries when you serve your dessert.)
5. Bake in the oven until dry, crisp, and white, about 1 1/2 hours. Change the position of your baking sheet half-way through and turn the heat down slightly if the meringues start to look brown.
6. To remove meringues slide parchment paper off the baking sheet. Cool and store in airtight container.

STRAWBERRIES

    2 boxes of strawberries (about 2 cups, after they have been quartered)
    2 tablespoons raspberry syrup
    2 tablespoons sparkling water
    1 tablespoon sugar
    1 tablespoon lemon juice

1. Clean the strawberries and cut into quarters. Rinse.
2. In a blender, blend 1/3 of the berries (about two cups), the syrup, sparkling water, sugar, and lemon juice.
3. Keep in a tightly closed container in the refrigerator until ready to serve.
4. Put the rest of the berries aside until ready to serve.

WHIPPED CREAM
    1 pint heavy whipping cream
    1 tablespoon vanilla sugar
        (or normal sugar)

1. Whip cream until it holds stiff peaks.

TO SERVE:
1. Pour the berries into the meringue bowls, top with whipped cream, and drizzle the strawberry puree over the top.
2. You can substitute chocolate syrup for the puree and/or raspberry yogurt for the whipped cream. You can put a tablespoon or two of cocoa powder into the whipped cream (or into the meringue) to make one or the other chocolate—or not. This is an immensely delicious and perfect valentine dessert.

Pride and Prejudice

Jane Austen

"Mr. Darcy, I am a very selfish creature; and, for the sake of giving relief to my own feelings, care not how much I may be wounding yours. I can no longer help thanking you for your unexampled kindness to my poor sister. Ever since I have known it, I have been most anxious to acknowledge to you how gratefully I feel it. Were it known to the rest of the family, I should not have merely my own gratitude to express."

"I am sorry, exceedingly sorry," replied Darcy, in a tone of surprise and emotion, "that you have ever been informed of what may, in a mistaken light, have given you uneasiness. I did not think Mrs. Gardiner was so little to be trusted."

"You must not blame my aunt. Lydia's thoughtlessness first betrayed to me that you had been concerned in the matter; and, of course, I could not rest till I knew the particulars. Let me thank you again and again, in the name of all my family, for that generous compassion which induced you to take so much trouble, and bear so many mortifications, for the sake of discovering them."

"If you *will* thank me," he replied, "let it be yourself alone. That the wish of giving happiness to you might add force to the other inducements which led me on, I shall not attempt to deny. But your *family* owe me nothing. Much as I respect them, I believe, I thought only of *you*."

Elizabeth was too much embarrassed to say a word. After a short pause, her companion added, "You are too generous to trifle with me. If your feelings are still what they were last April, tell me so at once. *My* affections and wishes are unchanged, but one word from you will silence me on this subject forever."

Elizabeth feeling all the more than common awkwardness and anxiety of his situation now forced herself to speak; and immediately, though not very fluently, gave him to understand that her sentiments had undergone so material a change, since the period to which he alluded, as to make her receive with gratitude and pleasure his present assurances. The happiness which this reply produced was such as he had probably never felt before; and he expressed himself on the occasion as sensibly and as warmly as a man violently in love can be supposed to do. Had Elizabeth been able to encounter his eye, she might have seen how well the expression of heartfelt delight, diffused over his face, became him; but though she could not look she could listen, and he told her of feelings, which, in proving of what importance she was to him, made his affection every moment more valuable.

They walked on, without knowing in what direction. There was too much to

329

be thought, and felt, and said, for attention to any other objects. She soon learned that they were indebted for their present good understanding to the efforts of his aunt, who *did* call on him in her return through London, and there relate her journey to Longbourn, its motive, and the substance of her conversation with Elizabeth; dwelling emphatically on every expression of the latter, which, in her ladyship's apprehension, peculiarly denoted her perverseness and assurance in the belief that such a relation must assist her endeavours to obtain that promise from her nephew which *she* had refused to give. But, unluckily for her ladyship, its effect had been exactly contrariwise.

"It taught me to hope," said he, "as I had scarcely ever allowed myself to hope before. I knew enough of your disposition to be certain that, had you been absolutely, irrevocably decided against me, you would have acknowledged it to Lady Catherine, frankly and openly."

Elizabeth coloured and laughed as she replied, "Yes, you know enough of my *frankness* to believe me capable of *that*. After abusing you so abominably to your face, I could have no scruple in abusing you to all your relations."

"What did you say of me that I did not deserve? For, though your accusations were ill-founded, formed on mistaken premises, my behaviour to you at the time had merited the severest reproof. It was unpardonable. I cannot think of it without abhorrence."

"We will not quarrel for the greater share of blame annexed to that evening," said Elizabeth. "The conduct of neither, if strictly examined, will be irreproachable; but since then, we have both, I hope, improved in civility."

"I cannot be so easily reconciled to myself. The recollection of what I then said, of my conduct, my manners, my expressions during the whole of it, is now, and has been many months, inexpressibly painful to me. Your reproof, so well applied, I shall never forget: 'had you behaved in a more gentlemanlike manner.' Those were your words. You know not, you can scarcely conceive, how they have tortured me; though it was some time, I confess, before I was reasonable enough to allow their justice."

"I was certainly very far from expecting them to make so strong an impression. I had not the smallest idea of their being ever felt in such a way."

"I can easily believe it. You thought me then devoid of every proper feeling, I am sure you did. The turn of your countenance I shall never forget, as you said that I could not have addressed you in any possible way that would induce you to accept me."

"Oh! do not repeat what I then said. These recollections will not do at all. I assure you that I have long been most heartily ashamed of it."

Darcy mentioned his letter. "Did it," said he, "did it *soon* make you think better of me? Did you, on reading it, give any credit to its contents?"

She explained what its effect on her had been, and how gradually all her former prejudices had been removed.

"I knew," said he, "that what I wrote must give you pain, but it was necessary. I hope you have destroyed the letter. There was one part especially, the opening of it, which I should dread your having the power of reading again. I can remember some expressions which might justly make you hate me."

"The letter shall certainly be burned, if you believe it essential to the preservation of my regard; but though we have both reason to think my opinions not

331

entirely unalterable, they are not, I hope, quite so easily changed as that implies."

"When I wrote that letter," replied Darcy, "I believed myself perfectly calm and cool, but I am since convinced that it was written in a dreadful bitterness of spirit."

"The letter, perhaps, began in bitterness, but it did not end so. The adieu is charity itself. But think no more of the letter. The feelings of the person who wrote and the person who received it, are now so widely different from what they were then that every unpleasant circumstance attending it ought to be forgotten. You must learn some of my philosophy. Think only of the past as its remembrance gives you pleasure."

"I cannot give you credit for any philosophy of the kind. *Your* retrospections must be so totally void of reproach that the contentment arising from them is not of philosophy, but what is much better,

of ignorance. But with *me*, it is not so. Painful recollections will intrude which cannot, which ought not to be repelled. I have been a selfish being all my life in practice, though not in principle. As a child I was taught what was *right*, but I was not taught to correct my temper. I was given good principles, but left to follow them in pride and conceit. Unfortunately an only son (for many years an only *child*) I was spoiled by my parents, who though good themselves (my father, particularly, all that was benevolent and amiable), allowed, encouraged, almost taught me to be selfish and overbearing, to care for none beyond my own family circle, to think meanly of all the rest of the world, to *wish* at least to think meanly of their sense and worth

compared with my own. Such I was from eight to eight and twenty; and such I might still have been but for you, dearest, loveliest Elizabeth! What do I not owe you! You taught me a lesson, hard indeed at first, but most advantageous. By you I was properly humbled. I came to you without a doubt of my reception. You showed me how insufficient were all my pretensions to please a woman worthy of being pleased."

"Had you then persuaded yourself that I should?"

"Indeed I had. What will you think of my vanity? I believed you to be wishing, expecting my addresses."

"My manners must have been in fault, but not intentionally I assure you, I never meant to deceive you, but my spirits might often lead me wrong. How you must have hated me after *that* evening?"

"Hate you! I was angry perhaps at first, but my anger soon began to take a

proper direction."

"I am almost afraid of asking what you thought of me when we met at Pemberley. You blamed me for coming?"

"No, indeed; I felt nothing but surprise."

"Your surprise could not be greater than *mine* in being noticed by you. My conscience told me that I deserved no extraordinary politeness, and I confess that I did not expect to receive *more* than my due."

"My object then," replied Darcy, "was to show you by every civility in my power that I was not so mean as to resent the past; and I hoped to obtain your forgiveness, to lessen your ill

opinion, by letting you see that your reproofs had been attended to. How soon any other wishes introduced themselves I can hardly tell, but I believe in about half an hour after I had seen you."

He then told her of Georgiana's delight in her acquaintance, and of her disappointment at its sudden interruption; which naturally leading to the cause of that interruption, she soon learned that his resolution of following her from Derbyshire in quest of her sister had been formed before he quitted the inn, and that his gravity and thoughtfulness there had arisen from no other struggles than what such a purpose must comprehend.

She expressed her gratitude again, but it was too painful a subject to each to be dwelt on farther.

After walking several miles in a leisurely manner, and too busy to know anything about it, they found at last, on examining their watches, that it was time to be at home.

"What could become of Mr. Bingley and Jane!" was a wonder which introduced the discussion of *their* affairs. Darcy was delighted with their engagement; his friend had given him the earliest information of it.

"I must ask whether you were surprised?" said Elizabeth.

"Not at all. When I went away, I felt that it would soon happen."

"That is to say, you had given your permission. I guessed as much." And though he exclaimed at the term, she found that it had been pretty much the case.

"On the evening before my going to London," said he, "I made a confession to him, which I believe I ought to have made long ago. I told him of all that had occurred to make my former interference in his affairs absurd and impertinent. His surprise was great. He had never

335

had the slightest suspicion. I told him, moreover, that I believed myself mistaken in supposing, as I had done, that your sister was indifferent to him; and as I could easily perceive that his attachment to her was unabated, I felt no doubt of their happiness together."

Elizabeth could not help smiling at his easy manner of directing his friend.

"Did you speak from your own observation," she said, "when you told him that my sister loved him, or merely from my information last spring?"

"From the former. I had narrowly observed her during the two visits which I had lately made her here; and I was convinced of her affection."

"And your assurance of it, I suppose, carried immediate conviction to him."

"It did. Bingley is most unaffectedly modest. his diffidence had prevented his depending on his own judgment in so anxious a case, but his reliance on mine made everything easy. I was obliged to confess one thing, which for a time, and not unjustly, offended him. I could not allow myself to conceal that your sister had been in town three months last winter, that I had known it, and purposely kept it from him. He was angry. But his anger, I am persuaded, lasted no longer than he remained in any doubt of your sister's sentiments. He has heartily forgiven me now."

Elizabeth longed to observe that Mr. Bingley had been a most delightful friend; so easily guided that his worth was invaluable; but she checked herself. She remembered that he had yet to learn to be laughed at, and it was rather too early to begin. In anticipating the happiness of Bingley, which of course was to be inferior only to his own, he continued the conversation till they reached the house. In the hall they parted.

My child—Star—you gaze at the stars,
and I wish I were the firmament that
I might watch you with many eyes.

— Plato

from the Journal of...
Queen Victoria

10 February 1840

Got up at a 1/4 to 9 —well, and having slept
well, and breakfasted at 1/2 p. 9. Mamma came
before and brought me a Nosegay of orange
flowers. My dearest kindest Lehzen gave me a
dear little ring... Had my hair dressed and
the wreath of orange flowers put on. Saw
Albert for the last time alone, as my
Bridegroom.

Saw Uncle, and Ernest whom dearest
Albert brought up. At 1/2 p. 12, I set off,
dearest Albert having gone before. I wore a
white satin gown with a very deep flounce of
Honiton lace, imitation of old. I wore my

Turkish diamond necklace and earrings, and Albert's beautiful sapphire brooch ... The Ceremony was very imposing, and fine and simple, and I think ought to make an everlasting impression on every one who promises at the Altar to keep what he or she promises. Dearest Albert repeated everything very distinctly. I felt so happy when the ring was put on, and by Albert. As soon as the Service was over, the Procession returned as it came, with the exception that my beloved Albert led me out. The applause was very great, in the Colour Court as we came through. Lord Melbourne good ... was very much affected during the Ceremony and at the applause ... I then returned to Buckingham Palace alone with Albert, they cheered us really most

342

warmly and heartily; the crowd was
immense, and the Hall at Buckingham Palace
was full of people, they cheered us again and
again ... I went and sat on the sofa in my
dressing-room with Albert; and we talked
together there from 10 m. to 2. till 20 m. p.
2. Then we went downstairs where all the
Company was assembled and went into the
dining-room —dearest Albert leading me in ...
Talked to all after the breakfast, and to Lord
Melbourne, whose fine coat I praised.

I went upstairs and undressed and put
on a white silk gown, trimmed with swans-
down, and a bonnet with orange flowers.
Albert went downstairs and undressed.

*

As soon as we arrived (at Windsor) we went to

343

our rooms; my large dressing room is our sitting room; the 3 little blue rooms are his ... After looking about our rooms for a little while, I went and changed my gown, and then came back to his small sitting room where dearest Albert was sitting and playing; he had put on his windsor coat; he took me on his knee, and kissed me and was so dear and kind. We had our dinner in our sitting room; but I had such a sick headache that I could eat nothing, and was obliged to lie down in the middle blue room for the remainder of the evening on the sofa; but ill or not, I never never spent such an evening. . . . He called me names of tenderness, I have never yet heard used to me before—was bliss beyond belief! Oh! this was the happiest day of my life!—May God

help me to do my duty as I ought and be worthy of such blessings.

11 February 1840

When day dawned (for we did not sleep much) and I beheld that beautiful angelic face by my side, it was more than I can express! He does look so beautiful in his shirt only, with his beautiful throat seen. We got up at 1/4 p. 8. When I had laced I went to dearest Albert's room, and we breakfasted together. He had a black velvet jacket on, without any neckcloth on, and looked more beautiful than it is possible for me to say... At 12, I walked out with my precious Angel, all alone—so delightful, on the Terrace and new Walk, arm in arm!... We talked a great deal together. We came home at one, and had luncheon soon after. Poor dear Albert felt sick and uncomfortable, and lay down in my room ... He looked so dear, lying there and dozing.

12. February 1840

Already the 2nd day since our marriage, his love and gentleness is beyond everything, and to kiss that dear soft cheek, to press my lips to his, is heavenly bliss. I feel a purer more unearthly feel than I ever did. Oh! was ever woman so blessed as I am.

13 February 1840

My dearest Albert put on my stockings for me. I went in and saw him shave; a great delight for me.

Great Britain's Queen Victoria married Albert, her mother's nephew and Prince of Saxe-Coburg Gotha, on February 10, 1840. They were happily married for 21 years.

I honor your gods
I drink at your well
I bring an undefended heart to
    our meeting place
I have no cherished outcome
I will not negotiate by withholding
I am not subject to disappointment

— Celtic vow

Credits

LITERATURE

Page 13: From *Open Secret: Versions of Rumi* translated by John Moyne and Coleman Barks, © 1984. Reprinted by arrangement with Shambhala Publications, Inc., Boston.

Page 16: Reprinted in the US, its territories and dependencies, the Philippines with the permission of Scribner, a Division of Simon and Schuster, Inc. from *The Collected Works of W.B. Yeats: Volume I: The Poems, revised* edited by Richard J. Finneran. NY: Scribner 1989. Reprinted in the world excluding the US by permission of A.P. Watt Ltd. on behalf of Michael B. Yeats.

Page 35: From *The Poetry of Robert Frost*, edited by Edward Connery Lathem, Copyright 1942, 1944 by Robert Frost. © 1970 by Lesley Frost Ballentine. Coyright 1916, © 1969 by Henry Holt and Company, LLC. Reprinted in the world and Canada by permission of Henry Holt and Company, LLC. Permission to reprint in the British Commonwealth excluding Canada granted by Random House UK on behalf of The Estate of Robert Frost, editor Edward Connery Lathem, and publisher Jonathan Cape.

Page 46: *Something's Gotta Give*, by Johnny Mercer © 1954, 1955 (Copyrights Renewed) WB Music Corp. All rights reserved. Used by permission of Warner Bros. Publications U.S. Inc., Miami, FL 33014.

Page 62: Copyright 1931, © 1959, 1991 by the Trustees for the E. E. Cummings Trust. Copyright © 1979 by George James Firmage, from *Complete Poems: 1904-1962* by E. E. Cummings, edited by George J. Firmage. Reprinted by permission of Liveright Publishing Corporation.

Page 72: Excerpt from *The Rainbow* by David Herbert Lawrence © 1943 by Frieda Lawrence. Published by Viking Penguin and reprinted by permission of Laurence Pollinger Limited and the Estate of Frieda Lawrence Ravagli.

Page 76: From *The Prophet* by Kahlil Gibran. Copyright © 1923 by Kahlil Gibran and renewed 1951 by Administrators C T A of Kahlil Gibran Estate and Mary G. Gibran. Reprinted in the US and elsewhere throughout the world (except Canada and the British Commonwealth) by permission of Alfred A Knopf, Inc. Authorization to reprint this quote in Canada and the British Commonwealth was granted by Gibran National Committee, P.O. Box 116-5487, Beirut, Lebanon, fax: (+961-1) 396916; email: k.gibran@cyberia.net.lb

Page 84: *Night and Day*, by Cole Porter © 1932 (Renewed) Warner Bros. Inc. All rights reserved. Used by permission of Warner Bros. Publications U.S. Inc., Miami, FL 33014.

Page 88: From *The Velveteen Rabbit*, © 1922 The Estate of Margery Williams, published by William Heinemann Ltd. and used with permission of Egmont Children's Books Limited, London.

Page 95: Reprinted courtesy of the Society of Authors as the literary representative of the Estate of John Middleton Murry.

Page 96: Reproduced courtesy of the Society of Authors as the literary representative of the Estate of Katherine Mansfield.

Page 111: From *Poems of the Sanskrit* (page 73), translated by John Brough (Penguin Classics, 1968). Copyright © 1968 by John Brough. Reprinted by permission of Penguin Books.

Page 112: Excerpts from *Winston and Clementine: The Personal Letters of the Churchills*. Copyright © The Lady Soames DBE 1998. Reprinted in the U.S. by permission of Houghton Mifflin Company. All rights reserved. Reproduced throughout the world excluding the US with permission of Curtis Brown Ltd., London, on behalf of the Estate of Sir Winston S. Churchill. Copyright the Estate of Sir Winston S. Churchill.

Page 116: From *Fairy Tales* by E. E. Cummings. Copyright © 1965, 1993 by the Trustees for the E. E. Cummings Trust. Reprinted by permission of Liveright Publishing Company.

Page 120: *I've Got You Under My Skin*, by Cole Porter © 1936 Chappell & Co. Copyright Renewed, Assigned to Robert H. Montgomery, Trustee of the Cole Porter Musical & Literary Property Trusts. Chappell & Co., owner of publication and allied rights throughout the World. All rights reserved. Used by permission of Warner Bros. Publications U.S. Inc., Miami, FL 33014.

Page 123: by William Carlos Williams, from *Collected Poems: 1909-1939, Volume I*. Copyright © 1938 by New Directions Publishing Corp.. Reprinted in the U.S. and Canada by permission of New Directions Publishing Corp. Reprinted in the world excluding the US and Canada by permission of Carcanet Press Limited.

Page 161: Reprinted with the permission of Scribner, a division of Simon and Schuster, Inc. from *The Collected Works of W.B. Yeats: Volume I: The Poems, Revised* edited by Richard J. Finneran. NY: Scribner 1989. Reprinted by permission of A.P. Watt Ltd. On behalf of Michael B. Yeats.

Page 166: From *The Love Poems of Rumi* by Deepak Chopra, MD Copyright © 1998 by Deepak Chopra. Reprinted by permission of Harmony Books, a division of Crown Publishers, Inc.

Page 173: Jung, Carl; *Collected Works, Vol. 17*. trans F.C. Hull. Reprinted by permission of Princeton University Press and Routledge.

Page 180: *I Only Have Eyes For You*, by Al Dubin and Harry Warren © 1934 (Renewed) Warner Bros. Inc. All rights reserved. Used by permission of Warner Bros. Publications U.S. Inc., Miami, FL 33014.

Page 182: *Revised Standard Version of the Bible*, © 1946, 1952, 1971 by the Division of Christian Education of the National Council of the Churches of Christ in the USA. Used by permission. All rights reserved.

Page 188: Courtesy of the Dance Collection, The New York Public Library for the Performing Arts, Astor, Lenox and Tilden Foundations.

Credits

351